Elements of Markets

Elements of Markets

Richard Perlman

The Dryden Press Inc.
Hinsdale, Illinois

Library of Congress Catalog Card Number: 71-188306
ISBN: 0-03-089127-2
Printed in the United States of America

Preface

The series of which this book is a part has been constructed on an assumption that we all hope is correct. The assumption is that undergraduate instruction, and specifically the teaching of economic principles courses is no longer the stepchild of university curricula. There are certainly signs that this assumption is correct. Younger instructors with career commitments to teaching *principles* as well as research and higher level instruction are being put in charge of principles teaching and the structure of the courses. This type of instructor finds the massive classic hardback text less than satisfactory for the needs of today's students. True, many of these paperweights have the advantage that they come in a neat package of instructor's manuals, study guides, test banks, programmed learning workbooks, graphics, film strips, etc., until hell won't have it—and neither will the conscientious instructor. The stuff is so pat, so canned, that any innovation on his part is lost in the shuffle or breaks the course program in a disruptive way. From the student's standpoint, the multi-revised, "up-to-date" denisons of the academic jungle are a real disaster. Their weight alone is enough to scare the average freshman or sophomore right into the nearest sociology course. When, and if, they actually start to read these jewels, students' original fear turns into sheer panic. I'll wager that there are more used economics principles texts with virtually uncreased spines than any other category of freshman course book.

There is nothing really startling in the series that we have put together. Our purpose has been to give an instructor some choices of material to be presented in the different segments of the principles course. To accomplish this, both the micro and macro portions have been divided somewhat arbitrarily into three segments each. Microeconomics has been split into *trade, markets,* and *microeconomic issues.* Macroeconomics has been divided into sections on *money, aggregates* or *macroeconomic analysis,* and *policy issues*. Within each of these six fields, three short paperback books have been prepared. The three books represent different approaches and different levels of difficulty. As you can see in the outline below, the lowest levels are all entitled "Elements of . . . ," the intermediate levels

MICROECONOMICS			MACROECONOMICS		
Trade	Markets	Issues	Money	Aggregates	Issues
1. Elements of Trade	1. Elements of Markets	1. Elements of Microeconomic Issues	1. Elements of Money	1. Elements of Macroeconomics	1. Elements of Economic Policy
2. Principles of Trade	2. Principles of Markets	2. Principles of Microeconomic Issues	2. Principles of Money	2. Principles of Macroeconomics	2. Principles of Economic Policy
3. Theory of Trade	3. Theory of Markets	3. Theory of Microeconomic Issues	3. Theory of Money	3. Theory of Macroeconomics	3. Theory of Economic Policy

"Principles of . . . ," and finally the highest levels "Theory of . . . ." This use of titles is designed to keep potential confusion between levels at a minimum.

Generally, books in the upper or "Theory" level are heavily analytical in approach and use algebra, geometry, and simple set theory. Books in the intermediate or "Principles" group are aimed at approximately the level of a standard principles text. Simple algebra and geometry are the most sophisticated tools of logic used. The lowest level uses only the very simplest geometry and descriptive material for development of the analysis. None of the books employ much institutional material nor present many straight facts and figures. This we leave to the instructor whose taste for his own materials is likely to be far more effective in teaching than any material we could include.

The whole idea of the series is to give the instructor a chance to *vary* the level of difficulty and method of approach between the several sections. Thus, for example, an instructor might choose the intermediate level for all phases of the course except *money*, where he might wish to use the higher level. We expect a great deal of substitution between the "Elements" and the "Principles" levels. Similarly, we expect a considerable amount of mixing between the "Principles" and "Theory." I doubt if there will be much mixing between the top and bottom levels within the same course although there is certainly nothing to prevent such a mix. Any six books chosen from each of the segments will make a coordinated package covering the complete range of a two semester principles course.

There is a certain amount of overlapping and repetition between the books, and this is intentional. In the first place, it is hoped that many of these books will fulfill the function of supplementing other materials in principles and intermediate courses. But even when used as primarily intended, the overlap provides emphasis and review of the most important concepts developed elsewhere.

In all of the books, there has been an attempt to keep the style as light as possible. Those that think that textbooks should read like journal articles will be very unhappy with this aspect of the series.

One of the key features of this approach is the fact that portions of the series can be quickly and economically revised as the contemporary scene dictates. The system employed by Dryden Press in producing this group of books makes it possible to go from manuscript to finished product in two months. We are living in a revolutionary age when it comes to the passing of information. The authors hope that our approach will take advantage of some of the potential this revolution makes possible. Obviously, your constructive comments will be most welcome. If this product is not exactly what you want, tell us. By maintaining close two-way communication, maybe we can all do a better job of developing a measure of understanding about the world of choices in which all of us, teachers and students, live.

A. J. Rogers, III
General Editor

Milwaukee, Wisconsin
December, 1971

Contents

Elements of Markets

Chapter One The Market System

Try to think of a world in which everything was free. We could get all the things we wanted—cars, shoes, bread, appendix removed, college education, etc.—for nothing. All our economic problems of earning and spending would be solved. We would have no use for money if the charge for everything were zero.

But who would produce all these things we would be "buying" at such bargain prices? Production requires our work effort; and for goods and services to be free, we would all have to work for nothing. But, in fact, if we didn't have to pay anything for the things we wanted, we wouldn't be likely to work at all for any wage, no matter how high, much less work for nothing.

Thus, nothing would be produced, and our happy costless dream world would fade into reality. The only goods that could be free would be gifts of nature which required no time nor effort to produce, and which were in such large supply that we all could get as much of them as we wanted at zero price. Older texts used to give the fresh air we breathe as an example of a free good. But we know better now. Waste from the goods firms produce, and even from our own consumption of them, pollute nature; and consequently, the cost of pure air rises above zero no matter who pays for it.

How about a walk around the block? At first view this seems to be a perfectly free good, if we broaden the concept of a good to include anything that gives us satisfaction. But economic thinking leads us to conclude that even this simplest of pastimes involves a cost. While taking the time for our walk, we are giving up doing something else—watching TV, reading a book, perhaps studying. The economist speaks of *opportunity cost* as the activity foregone while we do something else. We have already mentioned the opportunity cost of taking a walk. The opportunity cost of buying a \$100 bicycle is \$100 worth of the other things we could have done with that money. The opportunity cost of working on one job is the income we could have received from working on the next best job.

Thus, we get the sense of what economic reasoning is all about: economics is the study of choice among alternatives. At least this is the subject matter of economics at the unit level, whether it be of the individual producer or of the consumer of goods and services. This study is called *micro*economics to distinguish it from *macro*economics, which is concerned with the effect that the sum of individual decisions has on national or global economic conditions. How an individual worker will respond to a wage increase, whether he will want to work more or less, is a microeconomic problem; the effect of a general rise in wages on the price level, the levels of employment and unemployment, the foreign balance, are macroeconomic issues. This book is confined to a study of *micro*-economics; others in the series cover "macro" analysis and related topics—e.g., international trade, money and the banking system, determinants of national income.

Choice and Individual Decision-Making

We have to choose among alternatives because we do not have enough resources to get all the things we want. Since almost everything has a price tag on it, we consumers don't have enough money to buy without choosing among alternative goods.

To get money to buy products—a word we will use to include both goods and intangible services—we have to work. But work takes time and effort, and we have limited supplies of both. We need time off for rest and recreation, and have to choose between work time and free time knowing that less of the former gives us more opportunity for pleasure but less money to spend.

Thus, the spending unit has a choice among products it will buy and a choice as to how much time it will allocate to working to acquire money to spend. Note that we use the term "spending unit" instead of "individual" because spending and work is a group decision, with the group consisting of household members. Although households are usually composed of family members, for economic purposes the household is simply defined as the unit (sometimes consisting of only one person) that makes a joint decision on what will be bought and how much remunerative labor it will supply.

Economic analysis assumes that each household member has an equal vote on spending decisions, regardless of how much, if anything, he or she contributes to the household's spending power. Thus the needs and tastes of the child are given equal consideration to those of the working parent. In spending, the economically rational household tries to maximize the satisfaction it receives from its total purchases. Satisfaction is a vague term, broad enough to include need as well as pleasure; admittedly, there's not much fun in going to the dentist. The economist speaks of utility as the quality we seek in products. The utility of different products varies over time and circumstances. We derive more utility from a box of crayons when we are 5 than when we are 50, more utility from a good spare tire when we have a blowout on a desert road than when the car is in the garage.

As a supplier of work effort to earn money, the household also tries to maximize satisfaction. Here the choice is not a direct one involving the allocation of financial resources among alternative products; here the choice is between the pleasure of not working, of enjoying free time, and the satisfaction derived from spending power which the painful use of our time in gainful work will provide. Now, the economist frankly admist that the designation of work time as painful and free time as pleasurable oversimplifies reality. There is pleasure of varying degree in work, and we can think of a lot of things we have to do off the job which are more unpleasant than working.

But we can say, with little fear of contradiction, that on balance we have more fun off the job than on it. At least we have more voluntary choice in what we do with ourselves when not tied to job duties. This distinction–giving the nod to free time over working time in providing satisfaction–is enough to yield logical conclusions regarding the household's choice on the utilization of its time between the two.

Sometimes the household is unable to maximize its satisfaction in its allocation of time between free time and work time. Work schedules are often fixed, so that the individual worker only has the choice of accepting those schedules or not working at all. He can not select just that number of work hours which would lead to his optimum combination of the two classes of time. Then, too, the worker may not be able to find any work at all, or be forced to work only part time against his wishes. By their very nature, unemployment and underemployment imply that the workers hit are below their optimum choice of work time involvement.

The theories of consumer demand for particular products and of household labor supply satisfy one important aspect of meaningful theory in that they explain behavior. But they also contain one important shortcoming in that they are weak in contributing to our powers of prediction. We all have different tastes among goods and services–tastes which do not aggregate very well. Thus, although we can conclude that for most products a fall in price will lead to increased purchases, we cannot tell the extent of the increase for the individual consumer unless we know his preference pattern among all products. We are even more uncertain about the total worker response to a change in the earnings rate, much less the reaction of the individual worker.

The explanation of producer behavior in its maximization goal is stronger than that of the household, because it both explains the individual producer's choice among alternatives and predicts his reaction to a change in the determinants of production level. That is, it provides this information given the validity of the following two assumptions:

1. Production requires a given amount of time and effort from the firm's decision-making management; this time and effort does not vary with the level of production. Increasing output would require more men, materials, and perhaps machinery and even plants and equipment, but management works just as hard and long when business is slack as when it is booming. If we call worry work, running a business that isn't going

anywhere might put a heavier load on the bosses than managing a going concern. In any case, workers must put in more time to make more money, and machines wear out from strain; but management's hours do not relate to production figures.

2. The firm tries to maximize profits. This assumption is dependent on the first. Since profits are desirable, and it takes no more time or effort for the decision-maker to have the firm make more profits than less, the rational economic choice regarding profits is to maximize them.

This second assumption reads like a conclusion, which in fact it is, to some extent. The part that is a conclusion refers to the maximizing goal. The part that is an assumption is not the explicit, undeniable statement that profits are desirable, but the implicit view that profit-making takes precedence over other goals. The company may not charge the profit-maximizing price for its product because it might thereby kill off the competition and lay itself open to monopoly charges. New companies might not maximize profits in the short run because they would prefer to establish a reputation through increased volume. A firm may pay higher wages than necessary—note that profits depend on costs as well as revenues—to forestall unionization.

If profit maximizing is the economic goal of the firm, and our analysis will assume it is, the behavior of the firm with respect to its output and production policies becomes very simple. It will try to produce any output as cheaply as possible, using combinations of factors of production which achieve this result. Furthermore, given the price at which it sells its product, it will select that output which maximizes the difference between its revenues and costs.

Again, as in the condition of uncertainty that clouds the economic analysis of the household, if profit maximization were not the firm's goal, we could not predict the output and input policy of the firm unless we knew the order of priorities of its many goals. Even then, we could only explain and predict behavior on a firm-by-firm basis.

Markets and Pricing System

Once we have agreed that hardly anything is free, we should try to find out how prices are determined. Why does a car cost $4,000, and a piece of bubble gum a penny? You probably know the basis answer, which applies to most economic issues—it's simply a matter of supply and demand.

Supply refers to the offer for sale, at a price, of goods and services produced by business units, and the offer for wages of labor services by household workers. (There are other factors of production, used as inputs in production; but we are going to focus on labor, the most important factor, using as our criterion of importance its dollar contribution to total production and its role as a source of income. Moreover, almost all of us do or will work, but comparatively few of us will derive significant income from rent or interest or even profits.)

Demand refers to the quantity of goods and services household buyers will purchase at different prices to satisfy wants and needs, and the labor services producers will buy to use in production. Don't be confused because the word "services" appears in reference to both household and producer demand and supply. They are the same services, but seen from different viewpoints.

Take the example of an auto repair job at the local gas station. As a household member you demand the repair service, and there is nothing authoritative about your demand; it simply means that you are willing to pay a price for the job, and your dollars, not your exalted position in society, account for your demand being answered. The gas station is the business unit, or firm, that supplies the service, or repair job. Don't think that there is anything generous or charitable in supply; the word just indicates that the firm will provide the service at a price.

Now, the station hires mechanics to do its repair work. The mechanic *supplies* his services, his time and effort, his knowledge and skills to the station—again at a price, more familiarly known as a wage; and the station *demands* the mechanic's services, expressing that demand in the conventional way by paying him a wage.

What if the owner himself does the repair job? Then he doubles as manager and mechanic. In the former role, he supplies the service to the demanding customer. In the latter, he imputes a wage for his labor effort which, in effect, is hired by his firm. The reason he works on cars is that if the time he applies to his labor effort were devoted to administering the business, it would be worth less than the wages of the mechanic needed to replace him as a worker.

With goods, the relationship between supply and demand is clearer. The household demands goods supplied by producers. Whether considering the buying and selling of goods or services, one condition emerges as necessary for any transaction to occur. The price which the buyer will pay must equal the price which the seller will accept. In the case of the repair job, if the customer will pay only $70 for the job and the gas station will not do the job for less than $90, an impasse is reached. The work will not be done.

Now we know that except for auctions and similar styles of exchange, usually of a nonprofessional nature–such as an individual sale of used property by the owner to a prospective buyer, or the effort of a single buyer and single seller to arrive at a price for a product or productive service, as in a wage settlement reached by collective bargaining–prices are not arrived at by give and take negotiations between buyer and seller. In the case of the repair job, the customer probably does not say, "I'll go as high as $75," and the station concede to $85, and so on, until an agreement is reached. However, maybe there *is* a little of this give and take, and we shall see why shortly. For a better example of the absence of jockeying over price, you can go into a supermarket. There, if a price of $.25 is stamped on top of the can of soup you would like, you do not expect that through your power of persuasion you will get the checker to give you the soup for $.21.

We're switching examples here, so let's stay with the soup for awhile and return to the brake job later. We want to find out why the soup sells for just $.25. The individual buyer might be willing to pay $.30 for the can, but naturally he doesn't. The stamp markings tell him that the price he has to pay is only a quarter, and so he quietly and happily saves a nickel from what he would have been willing to spend if he were forced to. Similarly, the store might go as low as $.22 and still make what it considers a normal profit on the sale. But it doesn't give up the chance to make the three extra cents, because it feels it can sell the can for a quarter.

We say that both buyer and store know that the *market price* for soup is $.25. The *market price* is the price at which many buyers and sellers in the interaction of their demand and supply have arrived for the can of soup. Note that in this example we have assumed that the individual buyer and seller played no role in determining the market price; they just accepted it. If the buyer doesn't want to go as high as the quarter, he doesn't buy the soup; and if the store can't afford to charge only a quarter, it doesn't carry the product.

Extent of the Market

The buyer will pay only a quarter, if this is the market price, because he knows that he can conveniently buy the soup at this price elsewhere. The seller charges a quarter, not less, because he knows he can get all the buyers he wants at this price.

We mentioned convenience in setting geographical bounds to the market. If the soup sold for $.20 in another state, it would hardly pay the most careful shopper to travel many miles for this "bargain," even if he were to buy a lot of other groceries more cheaply at the same time. How about a lower price in another part of the city? This might be tempting for some shoppers, and certainly prices out of the neighborhood have some impact on the market price within it.

If we move closer, we find that stores within walking distance or an easy drive of each other will tend to sell the soup at the same price. Thus, the *market area* is defined as the geographical limits within which transactions tend to be made at the same price because of easy, low-cost access to alternative buyers and sellers. Forces on market price tend to become increasingly weaker the further removed they are from the market area under consideration. Thus the market price for soup in a south-side Chicago neighborhood is only slightly influenced by supply and demand conditions on the north side, and probably not touched by the level of soup prices in Milwaukee.

But some markets are world-wide in that transactions can be made by buyers and sellers anywhere with little or no extra cost. The market price for General Motors stock at any time is the same in Rome as it is in Nome. As long as a brokerage office is accessible, there is no inconvenience in trading in one place rather than another, even if the actual stock exchange on which issues are traded is located in New York City.

Transactions within a market do not need a physical market place to be carried out. In olden days this might have been necessary, and even today, in a few instances in our country and more generally in poorer countries, we have marketplaces where buyers congregate and sellers share overhead costs more inexpensively than if they each had their own establishment.

But intermediaries facilitate stock transactions to permit trading far beyond the limits of the Stock Exchange Building, and the market for cans of soup in a given location is just as real and strong with purchases and sales being made in dozens of separate stores as it would be if they were being made under one sprawling tent.

Determination of Market Price

Let's assume for the moment that the single buyer and store have nothing to say about the setting of the market price for soup. But let's try to find out why this market price is exactly a quarter. A customary approach in economics is to show that a condition could not be otherwise than as presented. Accordingly, we'll try to explain why the price of soup could not be other than a quarter, the actual market price.

Suppose the price were set below the market price—say, at $.20. At the lower price, there would be greater demand for the soup. Those who bought it at the higher price would now buy more cans in a given time period, and others who had been unwilling to buy at $.25 would now be attracted into the market by the lower price. On the supply side, some stores which had been willing to carry the soup at $.25 would find they could not sell it profitably at $.20, and would no longer carry the item—i.e., they would drop out of the supply side of the market.

The result, from both demand and supply reaction, is an excess of demand. The market would be out of balance, and pressure would be built up by demanders to bid up the price to the market level—the price at which the market *clears*, at which demand and supply are equal.

What if the price were initially set above the market price? Your sense of balance should enable you to figure out for yourself the adjustment towards market price. From what has been discussed so far, you get the picture of the general response of supply and demand to a change in price. The quantity demanded rises as prices fall and falls as prices rise, with opposite movements occurring in supply.

Economics makes frequent use of graphs to explain points. Since this is a beginning book, we will go easy on the graphs; but we should at least show the fundamental demand and supply curves. In fact, we will tell the market price story graphically in Figure 1.1.

The conventional downward sloping demand and upward sloping supply curves are drawn. We can read the quantity demanded and supplied off the graph at every price. At a price of $.20, demand is for *0B* cans of soup, and supply is only at *0A*. There is an excess of demand over supply of *AB* cans *(0B – 0A = AB)*.

The arrows along the curves show the direction of pressure on prices and the response of quantity, either of demand or of supply, to the price increase resulting from this pressure. Demanders bid up the price; and as they do so, some would-be demanders at the lower price drop out of the

Figure 1.1
Market Price for Soup.

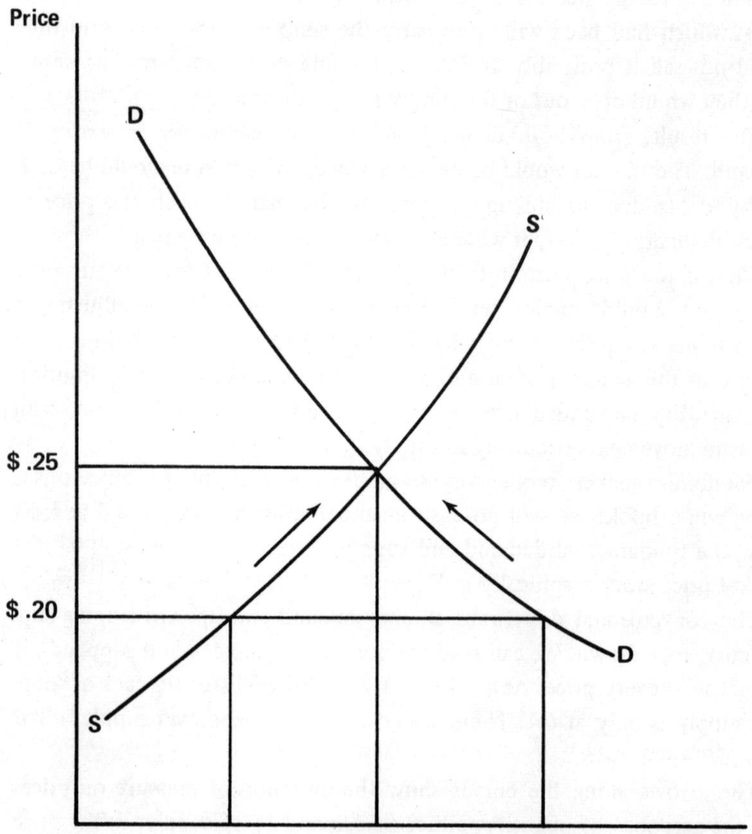

market. Supply expands as the price rises, and the excess demand dries up as the price of $.25 is reached. At this point the market clears.

The Role of Price in the Market System

Note the crucial part price plays in the market system. It is the regulator which moves supply and demand into balance. In our economy, price is the great rationer. If the market works smoothly and without interference, any tendency towards shortages or surpluses would be wiped out by counteracting price movements.

We might consider our demands insatiable, but that is only in the common sense of the word, not its economic meaning. Demand is only expressed through a willingness and ability to buy; and given our available supply of money, relative prices among different products determine where our demand will be applied. Thus, price allocates production to those fields where demand is felt. Production responds to the direction dictated by product demand. In a market economy, then, what is produced and how it is produced is determined by demand and supply, with price movements adjusting the two market components.

All economies are not run by market principles. In some, the consumer is not king, and production is directed by planners in keeping with national priorities set by authoritative rulers. Suppose a totalitarian regime decides to allocate production mainly to investment goods—transportation and communication facilities, power development, construction, and the like—and allows only a small amount of consumer good production—food, clothing, luxury goods, etc. At first view, it might seem that the market system could still operate. Because of low production, the price of consumer goods would skyrocket. Then price would play its role of rationing output.

There would be pressure to increase the supply of consumer goods. But we wouldn't have private determination of production, and the state would continue to thwart the pressure by limiting the allocation of productive resources to consumer good production. More seriously, many consumers would be squeezed out of the market for consumer necessities. Thus, a rationing system based on need rather than purchasing power would be introduced; it would limit demand to supply and keep prices down. A less cumbersome system would allocate substantial resources to consumer necessities, and simply let the prices of nonessentials rise.

But a market system means more than having markets clear through price movements. It also permits purchasing power to be exercised through consumer choice to determine the mix of production.

Even in our society, we sometimes deviate from a pure market system for many products. We make drugs illegal, and prevent the sale of liquor to minors. There are illegal transactions in these goods, but certainly at higher prices than if free consumer choice were expressed. We are not here advocating changing our social values—that's a political decision; we are merely pointing out that we don't always let the market operate.

Then there are a group of products that we feel are of such great personal value and need that we do not allow the price system to squeeze people with inadequate purchasing power out of the market. We provide for policing, fire protection, free or low-cost medical services to the needy, and, to a great extent, free education. These services are financed by (compulsory) taxes. We also compel children to attend school; thus, for education, both supply and demand are determined outside of the market system. We regulate transportation and communication services, keeping prices down and forcing adequate and sufficient service from producers to meet the high demand that results from relatively low prices.

Good and Bad Markets

So far, we have assumed that markets work smoothly with suppliers and demanders knowing the market price and deciding whether they will participate at that price. Let's go back to that consumer with brake trouble. He doesn't have perfect information on just how much the job should cost. He could go around to several stations pricing the job, but this takes a lot of time and, as a practical matter, he couldn't cover more than a few places. He isn't really sure of the market price, so we can say the market for brake jobs is not a good one.

The goodness or badness of a market is not a question of morality but of the knowledge of suppliers and demanders of market conditions—a knowledge which allows them to buy or sell on the best terms. Thus, goodness is related to the amount of information possessed. Lack of information does not presuppose a weak mentality. Sometimes the market conditions themselves are too uncertain to allow for accurate information. For example, in the labor market, compare the market for unskilled labor with the market for executives. The unskilled market is a good one. The worker knows what his job duties are; they are similar for different firms and even different industries. The wage, which is widely known, is his major consideration in deciding where he will work. From the employer's side, again the duties are well defined, and differences in the workers' capacities to perform them are either slight or, what is more important, of little influence on the firm's output. The wage within a given geographical area tends to be fairly uniform, and there is little need for much effort by intermediaries to bring supplier and demander together. Jobs can be secured by dropping into plants until a vacancy is found, by obtaining information on openings from friends or relatives, or by enlisting the efforts of the public employment service.

On the other hand, the market for executives is a bad one. The executive is not sure what his duties will be from one firm to the next; he knows they will be varied but difficult to write up. He has other interests in the job besides the pay rate—chances for advancement and promotion, possibilities of being transferred to other areas, and fringe benefits which might require an accountant to evaluate. In short, unlike the unskilled laborer, he is very uncertain of what his best job will be. From the employer's view, uncertainty regarding the best prospect is just as great. Ability difference among executives may be great, and it is usually crucial in affecting the firm's efficiency. What's more, the firm isn't even absolutely certain of what duties it wants the executive to perform. Therefore, the firm is unsure of who will best fit these important and high-paying jobs. References, testing, and extensive interviewing help in the decision, but intermediaries are often needed to aid the function of the market. Specialized private employment agencies with resources far beyond those available to the public employment service are often called on at substantial cost to aid the operation of the market in matching supply and demand.

Thus, bad markets usually require intermediaries to bring suppliers and demanders together to their mutual advantage. Good markets may require intermediaries to broaden transactions, but their role is less important in providing market information. A real estate broker operates in a very bad market in which buyer and seller might be thousands of dollars apart in their estimate of market price. The broker provides a vital service (for which he earns a high commission) in bringing them together by, in effect, informing them of market conditions.

But a stock broker operates in a very good market. Buyers and sellers know the exact market price at any given time, and ignorance of the price plays no part in the decision of whether to buy or sell a particular stock. The broker does receive a small commission for his work in assembling supply and demand orders, but he does not play a part in helping settle the current market price. That he gives advice on future market conditions and might thereby influence the market is another matter, one not related to his services in making today's market function.

Perfect and Imperfect Markets

Remember that in our discussion of the market for cans of soup we assumed that neither the buyer nor the seller had any influence on the market price. We treated them as price acceptors and not as price determiners. A market in which, say, the seller must passively accept the price is called a *perfectly competitive* market.

Let's take a closer look at these cans of soup. In doing so, we will have to take the edges off our assumption. We know from experience that an identical can may sell at different prices at various stores in the neighborhood. Right away, then, we know that the seller's market for soup is not perfectly competitive, but is instead somewhat *imperfect*. We know this because in a perfect market if the firm sold the can above the market price of $.25, its sales would fall to zero, with the other stores easily making up the lost sales of the high-priced store. Furthermore, if the store can sell all the soup it wants at the market price—a condition of perfect competition—it would be a foolish policy for it to sell a can at anything less than $.25.

If the cans of soup are identical, there must be something different about the stores to explain the variations in price. The store that sells at a higher price may offer credit, run more effective advertising, be conveniently located to a cluster of shoppers, make deliveries, stay open odd hours of the night, sweep the aisles more often, serve with a smile, and try every which way to accommodate the customer.

In effect, the store tries to create its own mini-market in which it can sell varying amounts depending on the price it charges, and does not have to operate on the all-or-nothing condition of perfect competition. Of course, it has to watch what the competition charges; its own individual market is greatly influenced by the price difference between what it and other stores charge for the same item. Customers like specialized services, but they aren't willing to pay too much for them in terms of higher prices.

Take the market for General Motors stock. If you want to sell your ten shares, you must accept the current market price. No one will pay more for them, and you don't have to sell them for less. You cannot individualize your shares by advertising that they have been carefully kept and are in good condition. Nobody cares. What if you had several thousand shares to sell? Then your offer might depress the market price, and you would no longer be able to operate as a price acceptor; the market would be temporarily imperfect.

Thus we see that perfection of competition within a market depends on the insignificance of the individual buyer or seller in the market. A seller is insignificant if he supplies only a small share of the market, as he would if he were a small seller of a standardized product.

Conversely, competition is imperfect when the individual seller, or buyer for that matter, contributes a signficant share of the market supply or demand. We speak of two categories of imperfection. In the first category, the market is imperfect and the individual firm important if it supplies a large share of the total market for a standardized product. Steel firms fit this description. There are a few large producers of a more or less identical product. When there are only a few large producers, we say the market is one of *oligopoly*, which is a word derived from the Greek meaning "few sellers." In the extreme case, where there is only one supplier, we speak of *monopoly*.

The second category consists of markets in which not necessarily large firms sell a dissimilar product. Here we speak of *product differentiation*. The market for soup fits this description. There are several companies making, say, vegetable soup. Each puts its brand name on the can, and this simple labeling practice differentiates the products somewhat. The companies also advertise, each emphasizing the better quality of its soup. From the retailing point of view, we have already mentioned how the stores try to differentiate their services. All in all, to the consumer, a product that was more or less the same among the several producers and sellers has become individualized. The result is that the market for cans of, say, vegetable soup has been to some degree individualized among the different brands, and even within the same brand. Thereby, competition is made imperfect; each seller now supplies a significant part of a fragmented market, and becomes a price determiner.

We find the same condition for perfect and imperfect markets in the factor market. A firm would hire labor in a perfectly competitive market if it were an unimportant user of the particular type of labor. It would buy in an imperfect market if it hired a great deal of the particular market's available labor of a given type. Then the market would be imperfect because of oligop*sony*(the last part of the word is Greek for buyer). A few large mills hiring much low skilled labor in a small community fits this description. In the extensive case, with only one buyer, there would be *monop*sony. It would be a rare situation indeed when one company hired *all* the labor.

As a counterpart to differentiation in the product market, the factor market would also be imperfect if firms hired even a small number of employees whose skills and productivity, though similar, showed a distinctly measurable variation. For example, take the case of executives. Most firms would find that they hired a large share of the available executives possessing just the specific skills and aptitudes the company was seeking.

Scope of the Book

In the following chapters, we are going to study both the factor market and the product market, and consider conditions of perfect and imperfect competition. As has been explained in the previous discussion, these markets are interrelated. For example, households demand goods from the product market and supply labor services to the factor market. In Figure 1.2, we show the full interrelationship. The double arrows connect the demand and supply components for each market. Households supply other factors to firms–capital and land–and firms use factors other than labor–materials, machinery, equipment, and land. But in this short book, we'll just stress the labor market.

Figure 1.2
Components of Product and Factor Markets.

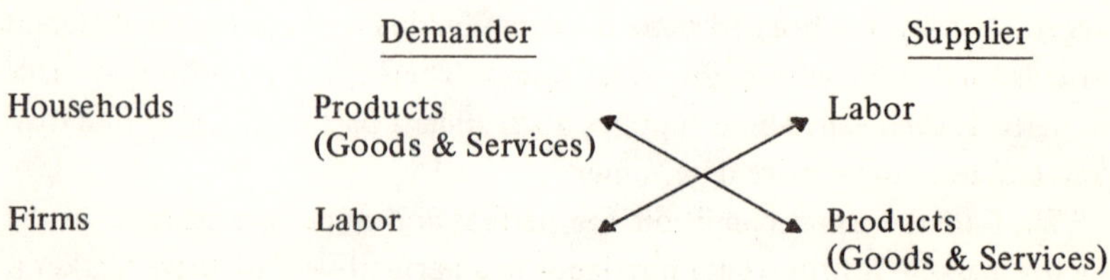

There are two possible approaches to our study. We could treat each market separately, but then we would be switching from household to firm decisions twice. Alternatively, we can follow the conventional method of studying each economic unit at a time–first the household, then the firm. This has the advantage of following through the complete market behavior of an economic unit, but has the disadvantage of having only half of each market discussed at a time. Well, you can't have everything.

The next chapter, dealing with consumer demand for products, is perhaps the segment of greatest interest to all of us in that it explains what we do with our money, given existing prices and our own household income. In the third chapter, we will study our decision with regard to how much we will earn–to the extent that we have that choice–in terms of how much we will work. This chapter also contains a few words about our decision on what occupation we will follow.

The last two chapters move on to a discussion of the economic behavior of the firm. The fourth chapter explains what amount of a given product the firm will supply, given the nature of demand for the product, the degree of competition for it in the market, and the price at which the firm can sell its output. The fifth and last chapter, on the firm's demand for labor, deals with the assumption that the firm will strive to maximize its profits by producing any output as cheaply as possible. This means that the firm must consider not only the cost of labor but also the cost of the factors of production. In addition, it must take into account the efficiency in production of the individual factors it uses, how well they work in combination, and how easily the factors can substitute for each other. This might be the most complicated chapter, but you will have had plenty of practice in economic reasoning before you get to it.

Chapter Two The Household as Consumer

Economists agree that the basic purpose of all economic activity is consumption. If you are going to accept this view, it would be a good idea to know just what is meant by consumption. In economic usage, *consumption* is simply the using up of goods and services. We buy products so we can use them. We wish they would last forever, and in fact some goods do stay with us for a considerable length of time after we've bought them. We would be very disturbed if a house we bought became a completely worthless wreck within a year.

We call those goods which yield their benefits slowly *investment goods* or in the case of goods bought by households, *consumer durables.*[1] But whatever the lifespan of the goods we buy—whether it be a ride on a roller coaster that is consumed instantaneously, a refrigerator that lasts 10 years, or a house that lasts 50—the reason for our purchase is eventually to consume the product bought.

Even when we decide not to consume—that is, decide to save some of our spending power—we can consider these savings as the choice of future consumption over current consumption, whether by ourselves or, in the case of saving to build an estate, by our heirs.

Consumers buy in order to consume, and work in order to obtain the wherewithal to consume. Firms produce goods to earn profits and satisfy consumption goals of profit makers. In this chapter, we are interested only in the individual consumption choice. Our study is narrowed even further when we confine it to household choice among alternative products, leaving to the book on macroeconomics the broader question of the determinants of the total level of consumption.

The household—the basic spending unit, whether or not its members are joined by family ties—takes into account the needs and wants of all its members in its consumption decision. As we mentioned before, demand for consumption needs and wants may be insatiable; but for demand to be effective and to have economic meaning, it must be backed up by spending power. Thus, we can say that demand is nothing more than the quantity of products we will buy related to how much of our purchasing power it will take to buy them. This last is best explained by the prices of the particular things we buy. Our total demand is obviously closely related to our spending power, which in turn is mostly determined by our income.

The Effect of Income on Demand

Although price relationships between goods are the major determinants of the particular goods and services we buy, our spending power limits the total amount of all goods we buy. We think of the financial resources that we will use for buying things in terms of a time period. How much can we spend in a week, a month, a year?

[1] Technically, an investment good is defined quite arbitrarily as one that will take longer than a year to be fully consumed. In national production accounting data, again quite arbitrarily, we include houses as household investment purchases. All other household purchases with a long consumption life are called consumer durables.

Let's look at a month's expenditures on goods and services. The main ingredient in our purchasing power during the month is the amount of money we earn for the month. This is our *income*. If we use up all our income in the purchase of consumption goods, which in turn yield all their benefits during the month, then we will be in the same financial shape at the end of the month as we were in the beginning. That's the way most of us live anyway, just breaking even. The average household takes home about $700 a month, and manages quite easily to spend it all with nothing to show for it afterward—except perhaps the hopeful experience of having gone through the month without losing ground. (That isn't $700 per wage earner, but $700 per total household work effort; about half the households have more than one worker.)

We have other sources of buying power during the month, too. We can borrow money either directly or indirectly by buying on credit. Unlike the federal government, however, we have limitations on our borrowing power. In these days of easy credit (even if at high interest rates), we can go through most of our lives in debt. But once we reach our debt limit, repayment of loans must equal new borrowing; so we can't use debt financing as a net addition to our buying power. For example, if the household has a debt limit of $1,000 which it has reached, it has to pay off, say, $80 a month, and can only borrow 80 additional dollars, if we omit interest. Thus continued borrowing capacity allows the household to keep its debt intact, but leaves nothing as a contribution to buying power.

Some households are lucky enough to have assets which can contribute to spending power during the month. It has acquired these assets, if not through gifts or inheritance, from the simple but usually painful process of not consuming all its income over the years. Accumulated assets represent the household's wealth. This is a quantity of value that can be expressed in dollars and cents whatever its form—whether it be liquid in the form of cash or securities that could be easily turned into spending power, or illiquid in the form of equity in a house or furnishings that would be hard to change into money quickly.

Theoretically, the household could liquidate all its assets and spend this money during the month; so if it had $3,000 in assets and $700 in earnings, it would have $3,700 in spending power for one month. But most households don't budget this way. Slowly accumulated assets are not considered expendable during a given month. Of course, we can think of household emergencies—serious illness for example—that might require liquidation of some or all assets; but for normal monthly outlays, the typical household does not put its assets into its market demand. Nevertheless, the size of these assets certainly does affect the level of monthly consumption demand. Apart from the income from earning assets—that is, interest, rent, and dividend income—the greater a household's assets the more it will tend to spend, if for no other reason than the reduced incentive it will have to add to these assets through saving.

Since addition to buying power through borrowing is limited, and since most households don't hold substantial liquid assets or, what is more important, don't like to reduce them for current consumption purposes, by far the major determinant of spending on consumption is the income from work earnings by household members.

The major relationship between income and consumption expenditure is really quite a simple one. All that holds us down from buying more is our limited flow of funds; so the greater our flow of income, the more we spend on consumption goods. When the flow becomes a trickle, because of bad times in general or because of economic misfortune localized to particular households, expenditures fall.

While we spend more in total on consumption, the higher our income the more our pattern of purchases tends to change. We buy a lot more of some goods, a little more of others, and in a few cases we might even buy less.

Before we examine the response of consumption of particular classes of products to rising income, let's look at the budget or *level* of consumption distribution of our typical $700-a-month household. Budget studies show an average of about $200 a month going to food and beverages. If there are four members in the household—and that's about the usual size for households having more than one member—this averages out to about $.55 per meal per person, assuming no snacks. This obviously doesn't provide for gracious dining, or even heavy drinking. There's no need to detail the entire typical budget, except perhaps to note a few other big items. The household will probably spend about $150 a month on housing, including utilities and furnishing, and about $60 a month on the family car, including repairs, maintenance, depreciation, insurance, parking fees (if any), and licenses. Without going through the entire list, we can see that there isn't much left for luxuries. Let's not even talk about savings.

Now suppose the household income rises substantially—maybe because the chief breadwinner gets a big raise or a better job, or because the wife gets a job. It doesn't really matter what the cause, as long as we consider that expenditures will still be shared and that the group feels that this higher income will prevail indefinitely, so that it can adjust its consumption upward without worry that it will soon have to go through the painful process of downward readjustment.

At the higher income level, the household will tend to spend more on food. Meals will be more varied, gourmet dishes will creep into the diet, and there might even be some eating out, with market labor doing the cooking and serving instead of the "free" labor of the housewife. But eating has its limitations; food is a necessity, and its luxury aspects are quite peripheral for most of us. What is more, our society does not measure prestige by an ample waistline. We will spend more on food as our income rises, but certainly food expenses will take a declining share of each additional $1,000 of income. We can say that food, and for that matter all necessities, are income insensitive; this means that changes (increases) in income only slightly alter (raise) our consumption of them. After all, in the strict meaning of the word "necessity," we would try to buy a given required amount no matter how low our income; and we would not derive added satisfaction from acquiring an overabundance. It is only because food has some luxury aspects beyond caloric or nutritional values that we consider our expenditures on this item at all after our income rises above levels that satisfy basic needs. For an extreme example of income insensitivity of a necessity, consider diabetics. When their income rises, they do not increase their daily insulin dosages.

But luxuries are another matter. They add flavor to life, and are excluded from purchases only because of income limitations. As income rises, we spend more and more on amusement, recreation, travel, and all the things we couldn't afford before. Luxuries are income sensitive; out of each additional $1,000 (or, theoretically, $1.00) we earn, we spend a growing share on luxuries.

What about savings? Certainly, the pressure of necessity prevents savings at low incomes; but as our incomes rise, although we may wish to defer consumption by saving part of our current income, we are lured into spending by the availability of luxuries which we can now afford. On balance, the forces of current demand and the desire for providing for future consumption—especially in later years when earnings may not be as high—tend to balance out. On the average, the share of additional dollars of income going to savings tends to remain more or less constant at a rate of about 10 percent.

For all broad classes of goods, consumption rises with income; however, it does so at different paces, depending on whether a class is composed of luxuries or necessities. But within classes, substantial substitution tends to take place. Look at the household food budget: rising income allows a substitution of more desirable but expensive protein for starches, and within the meat subclass, steak for hamburger. Thus for individual items which form part of low-income budgets, a rise in income might result in an absolute reduction in purchases. These low-income products are called *inferior goods*. Potatoes are probably an inferior good.

We can even relate family size and population trends to income. In our urban-suburban society, children are mainly consumption goods. Unlike the children in farm economies, city children contribute nothing to current income, but they consume a great deal. They do contribute indirectly in later life to the support of older parents through taxes in support of social welfare programs, but not many would argue that this indirect future support provides strong motivation for individual parents to increase family size.

As a consumption good, children have a substantial luxury aspect. A rise in income tends to lead to an increase in expenditures on children, at about a constant share of the extra income. The expenditure on each child rises; at a higher income level, more is spent on children's education, amusement, and recreation, as well as on the luxury aspects of necessities—e.g., varied diet, better clothes, more housing space.

If, on balance, consumption relating to children fits the consumer luxury category (as it probably does in advanced economies), expenditures per child rise faster than income. Then, if the total expense of children takes a constant share of income, families will tend to have fewer children the higher their income. On a broad national basis, this behavior helps explain the higher birth rates of poor countries as compared to wealthier ones.

Effect of Tastes on Consumption

All households will tend to consume more as their income rises. However, at any given level of income, individual households will differ widely in their choice of purchases. We say the households differ in *taste*. Sometimes taste in the economic sense of the word differs from the usual meaning of preference, in that, economically speaking, tastes are more dictated by necessity than by freely chosen preference. A family with eight children has a greater "taste" for expenditure on food consumption than does a childless couple.

In its broadest sense, taste can also explain differences in total consumption expenditures among households of the same size earning the same income. One household may consume much less than the average in its economic class, because it has a strong taste for future spending power and will save more.

While taste for any goods differs widely among individual households, the taste of all tends to move in the same direction when a new product is devised which performs the service of an old one more effectively. Home consumption of oil for heating replaced coal, and later gas took away some of the oil market. Tastes can also be manipulated. This is especially true of fashions. Women's hemlines go up and down, depending on the current creative inclination of leading designers. Whatever the motivation of the fashion leaders, the suppliers are pleased with any measures that build in early obsolescence in the product they sell. Tastes have probably been somewhat deflected away from cigarettes by continual health warnings about excessive smoking.

Effect of Prices of Substitutes on Demand

Recall the nature of opportunity cost, which was explained at the very outset of this book as the value of an activity foregone to engage in the present one. Activity is a purposely loose term that includes any economic decision. It applies to consumption as well. When we buy good A, we forego the opportunity to buy an equal dollar value of goods B, and/or C, and/or D, etc., and/or the opportunity to save the money instead. But the next best alternative for the good we actually buy is a close substitute for it in satisfying a consumption want.

A tried and true textbook example of close substitutes is butter and oleo. Let's look at the case with the demand for butter in mind. Buying butter leaves a certain amount of oleo unbought. Let's say the household decided on the purchase of butter instead of oleo because at current prices its preference for butter over oleo exceeded the financial sacrifice needed to acquire it.

Now, suppose the price of oleo were to fall. The reason for the drop doesn't matter as long as we rule out a switch away from oleo because of changing tastes or higher income by the consumer. That is, we assume that the price fell because of a more plentiful supply. The result of this drop in the price of oleo is to raise the opportunity cost of butter. Before, with butter, say, at \$.60 per pound and oleo at \$.40 per pound, the typical consumer just about preferred the butter; now, if the price of oleo fell to $.30 a pound, and the household liked its weekly pound of butter just a little more than 1 1/2 times ($.60/$.40 = 1 1/2) the same amount of oleo, butter would no longer be a good buy for it. The relative financial outlay against butter would be greater than the household's relative preference for butter. It would now pay the household to buy the oleo, and use the $.30 saved to buy other things, thus increasing its total satisfaction. Economists try to shy away from numerical measurement of utility; but if, with this $.30, the household can buy something that gives it half the satisfaction of butter, this satisfaction added to the pound of oleo, which gives it almost 2/3 the utility of butter, yields greater total utility than would the outlay of $.60 for butter.

Thus, a fall in the price of a substitute weakens the demand for a given product for the individual household and consequently for the market as a whole. Market price would tend to fall, as the total quantity demanded fell. Similarly, if the price of substitutes rose, the demand for the product in question would rise.

Some goods are not substitutes for other goods, but are just the opposite in that they are demanded jointly. These goods are called *complements*. Steak is a complement for steak sauce, bread for butter, automobiles for tires. The reader can apply his own reasoning power to explain why the demand for a product falls if the price of its complement rises.

So far, we have discussed the three main factors that influence the level of consumption demand for any product–income, tastes, and the price of substitutes. To summarize our conclusions, demand is heavier the higher our income (except for a few goods), the stronger our taste for the product, the higher the price of substitutes (the lower the price of complements). We should now explain why a household–given its income and tastes and a constant price of other goods, especially substitutes–demands a certain number of units of a product per time period.

Household Demand at Market Price

Let's use our soup example of the last chapter to explain how many units (cans) the household will buy in a week at the market price of $.25. First of all, we must assume that the household can derive some satisfaction (utility) from soup, or it wouldn't buy any at all. There is no need to assume that the household is crazy about soup, just that it would be willing to buy some if the price were right.

To start the analysis, suppose the household were to buy four cans a week. If the fourth can gave as much utility as anything else the household could do with a quarter, it would weight the decision to buy a fifth one. Older economic analysis used to introduce the concept of *decreasing marginal utility* here, claiming that the fifth, or marginal, can gave less added utility than the fourth can, because our taste for soup would tend toward satiety as we drank more and more of it. The argument would then lead to the conclusion that the fifth one would not be bought, because it would give less satisfaction than a quarter spent on other things.

Modern economic thinking does not require that a product be characterized by decreasing marginal utility to explain the household's equilibrium quantity demanded—that quantity for which the satisfaction from the last dollar spent gave as much utility as could be derived from a dollar spent on other things. This is not to deny the fact that marginal utility for the soup might decline as we consume more of it during a week, but only to claim that it is not necessary to assume that it does. We may think of demand in relative terms, considering the utility that could have been derived from alternative purchases. If we were to buy the fifth can of soup, then the \$.25 spent on this purchase could neither be spent on something else nor saved. What stops us from buying more than four cans is not that the additional soup necessarity gives us less satisfaction, but that the satisfaction gained from the \$.25 spent on the extra can is less than the satisfaction foregone by taking \$.25 away from some other use.

Whatever method we use to explain the level of purchases, rational household decisions based on the goal of utility maximization require that the last dollar spent on all products gives equal utility. If it does not, we can increase our total utility by switching one or more dollars away from their current use. In our example, the household buys exactly four cans per week because the utility of the fourth can yields as much and no more satisfaction as could be obtained from \$.25 spent elsewhere. If it buys four cans at \$.25, how many cans would the household buy at \$.20? How many would it buy at any price? When we have answered this last question, we have explained the form of the household's demand curve for soup—the relationship of quantity demanded to price.

Derivation of Household Demand Curve

By the demand curve, or schedule, for a product, we mean the quantity that would be demanded at different prices at a given time. The momentary nature of the demand curve permits study of the household's response to a change in product price alone, with income, tastes, and the price of substitutes remaining constant.

Since this is not a mystery book (we hope), let's jump to our conclusion as to the pattern of this response, and then explain the forces that lead us to this conclusion. *For almost all goods, a fall in price will lead to an increase in quantity demanded, and a rise in price will lead to a decrease in quantity demanded.* You met this conclusion before in the last chapter, but now we can discuss the factors–specifically, substitution and income aspects of demand–that allow more precision in our explanation of this observable behavior.

Substitition Effect

When the price of a product falls, the price of other goods remaining constant, it becomes cheaper than the other goods. The relative cheapness of the good in question encourages the substitution of this good for its substitutes. Let us analyze this process of substitution through the use of an example, assuming that consumer demand was in equilibrium before the price decline.

Take the case of individual household demand for pounds of steak per week. We are, of course, dealing with a household that is well enough off to buy steak at all. Suppose the household is at its equilibrium demand at 48 ounces, consumed at a price of $.09 per ounce. We know steak isn't sold by the ounce, at least not yet. But let prices keep going up and who knows how minute the units of sale might become. In any case, we are dealing with ounces here to allow for the realistically small changes in quantity demanded that would follow a price decline.

Now, recall what we mean when we say that the household is at equilibrium with a $4.32 purchase of steak per week (48 ounces at $.09 per ounce). The last penny spent on steak gives as much satisfaction as could be derived from the penny put to any other use. Again, if the household is in complete consumption equilibrium, the satisfaction gained from the last penny spent on all things it buys is the same.

Let the price of steak fall to $.08 per ounce. If the household does not change its quantity demanded, it will be spending only $3.84 a week on steak instead of $4.32. Steak has now become relatively cheaper than other products. The household's taste for steak hasn't changed, but it can now get more of it for its three-hundred-and-eighty-fifth cent–which is another way of saying that its 49th ounce would cost less. The household would no longer be in consumption equilibrium. The satisfaction gained from the last penny spent on steak, with tastes constant, would be greater than what could have been obtained had that penny been spent on something else. This conclusion is reached, as long as additional steak yields any positive utility at all, simply because more steak can be bought with the last penny.

To restore its consumption expenditures to equilibrium, the household will have to *substitute* steak for other things in its total weekly purchases. It will want to buy more steak until the extra utility from the last penny spent on steak once more equals the utility from the last penny spent on all things. Recall that to restore the balance, it is not necessary for total satisfaction in steak to decline as more is consumed, because as less of other things are bought, especially of foods, their marginal utility will tend to rise. But, in any case, the quantity of steak purchased in response to the *substitution effect* of a decline in price will be increased by the rational, satisfaction-maximizing household.

Income Effect

At the same time steak tends to be substituted for other foods, another effect works to reinforce the substitution effect, leading to an increase in the quantity demanded at the lower price. Recall that buying the same amount of steak would reduce the outlay from $4.32 to $3.84 per week. Although the household's money income hasn't changed, it now has more money to spend on everything if it still only buys the same amount of steak as before. Forty-eight cents is not a big windfall, but it does represent an *income effect* from a price reduction of a particular product. Obviously, the potential size of the income effect depends on the initial importance of the product in the household's budget. Except for athletes and those with very high incomes, steak as a general rule, would not constitute an important part of household budgets. But the actual size of the income effect depends on the income sensitivity of demand for the product in question. Steak is a luxury food. Consequently, it is income sensitive. That the income effect from a price decline might not be greatly felt is not because households don't increase their purchases of steak significantly when income rises, but because the total *real* gain in income from a price decline in an unimportant budget item is small.

But no matter how small, the income effect from the price decline of steak reinforces the substitution effect, and both lead to an increase in the quantity of steak demanded at a lower price. For most goods, income and substitution effects work in the same direction; therefore, the demand curve, pictured in Figure 1.1, sloping downward, with quantity moving in opposite direction to price, applies.

In the case of a few goods, though, the income effect opposes the substitution effect. That is, as incomes rise, we buy less of such goods. As you recall, we claimed that food was income insensitive; as income rose, the share of the budget going to food would decline. But this does not mean that total expenditures on food would fall as income rose; it simply means that out of each additional dollar of income the *increase* in total food expenditures would tend to decline. Food is still a *normal* good in that a rise in income would increase total expenditures, albeit slightly and at a declining rate, on the good.

Broad classifications of products tend to be normal simply because it is difficult to substitute *between* classes, no matter how our tastes differ at different income levels. It is hard to substitute clothes or recreation and amusement expenses for food to any great extent. But *within* classifications substitution is more practical; and as our incomes rise, we can cater to our more expensive tastes. Hence, there are some foods that are undoubtedly *inferior* goods, in that if our income rose we would buy less of them. As we said earlier, potatoes fit this description of an inferior good.

For a good of this type, the income effect of a price decline goes counter to the substitution effect. If potatoes fell, say, by $.03 a pound, the household would have a real gain in its purchasing power to the extent that potatoes entered into its weekly budget. The increased spending power would direct demand away from potatoes. But remember that the substitution effect, resulting from the cheaper price for potatoes, still acts to increase the quantity demanded at a lower price. Thus, if potatoes were but a small part of the household's budget, the substitution effect would outweigh the negative income effect and lead to a conventional, downward sloping demand curve.

It is easy to see, then, why only a few goods would ever have perverse demand curves—perversity being defined as the situation that exists when the quantity demanded moves in the same direction as the price change. In the first place, the good must be an inferior one; and this would only apply to some particular subgroups within broad consumption necessity classifications. Then, the income effect would have to be very strong, meaning that the subgroup would have to form an important part of the consumer's total budget. Obviously, the narrower the subgroup, the less likely this will be the case. Perhaps, in poor societies, potatoes fit these requirements. The overall economy would have to be weak; in high income countries, this cheap food would not take a large share of the average household's budget. All in all, if we consider our demand curves as downward sloping, especially in our country, we include all products except a few which might be considered economic curiosities.

Market Demand

So far, we have been speaking of the individual, or typical, household demand for a product. But each spending unit buys only a minute share of the total market. Nevertheless, it is an easy step to move from individual households to total market demand for a product.

The market demand is simply the sum of the demand of each household at different price levels. The total quantity demanded is subject to two influences: (1) changes in quantity demanded by each buying household as the price changes, and (2) buyers' entry into and exit from the market as the price falls and rises, respectively.

Let's take the case of steak. As the price falls, those households which bought some steak at the higher price will increase their scale of weekly purchases. At the same time, households which previously could not "afford" to buy steak will enter the market and add to the total market demand at the lower price. (Opposite individual and total responses would be made to a price increase.)

We are now in a position to put precise economic reasoning into the expression "can't afford to buy steak." Realistically, steak can't be bought in very small units–say, an ounce. Let's say that one pound a week is the least a household can buy from a foodstore. If household income is low, it will find that the utility from $1.44 (one pound at $.09 an ounce) worth of steak is not as great as the utility from the $1.44 spent on other things. It is not that this household has a lower preference or taste for steak than higher income households; but after its limited budget is spread among necessities and perhaps a luxury or two, it has not acquired enough of these other things to reduce the marginal satisfaction from the last $1.44 spent on any of them to the utility from the first pound of steak. If the price falls to $.08 an ounce, some households will find that they can now "afford" steak and will enter the market as demanders. Here, the satisfaction, or utility, derived from the first pound of steak exceeds that which could be obtained from applying the $1.28 per week to anything else. The market for steak expands on the demand side as new entrants appear in response to the lower price.

Sometimes a very wide difference appears between individual household and market demand for a product. This is especially true for cases in which the individual demand is price insensitive but the effect of price movements on the number of household demanders is great. Take the example of the evening newspaper. The single household will not alter its quantity demanded at all if the price should change. In effect, it makes an all or nothing decision, buying one copy or none depending on the price. Even the most avid bargain hunter is unlikely to buy two papers instead of one, if the price should fall. But at a lower price, many households which were not in the market before would enter to buy a copy. Similarly, if the price rose, some households would drop out of the market, while those remaining would not buy fewer papers; they don't sell newspapers by the section. Thus, the market demand curve for newspapers follows the conventional downward sloping path, even if the one for the individual household has a peculiar shape—a vertical line from one unit out on the X-axis (quantity axis) up to the height (price) at which it will decide not to buy the paper.

Changes in Demand

A demand schedule relates the quantity demand to the price of the product. The curve presents an instantaneous picture of the reaction of quantity demanded to different prices, with all influences other than price remaining constant. We know that the elements that determine the price-quantity relationship at any *one* time—income, tastes, price substitutes—may change, and change widely over time. But these changes in the basic determinants of the demand curve are not reflected in the moment-of-time demand schedule, or curve, which isolates the price influence on quantity demanded.

Thus, any change in the demand curve, or change—increase or decrease—in demand, results only from a change in one or more of the three fundamental determinants of demand. As we noted before, there will be an increase in demand if incomes rise, and/or tastes for the good in question strengthen, and/or the price of substitutes rises. This increase in demand should not be confused with an increase in the *quantity* demanded in response to a decline in price, which represents a downward movement along a given demand curve and not a movement to a new curve.

Let's expand on this difference by referring to our previous example of the demand for steak. Compared with the situation 20 years ago, the price of steak is much higher and the average household consumption of it has also gone up a great deal. If we did not realize there has been an increase in demand for steak mainly as a result of an increase in one of the fundamental determinants of demand at any time, namely, income, we would erroneously conclude that steak was one of those peculiar goods which shows an increase in quantity demanded as its price rises.

In Figure 2.1, we show graphically the actual changes that have occurred. Twenty years ago, the market price for a pound of steak was at P along demand curve D. Of course, market price is not determined by demand alone, but we are not yet in a position to discuss supply schedules. All we need to say here is that the market clears at P, meaning that the supply schedule crosses D at this point.

Now over the years, there has been an increase in demand for steak because of rising income. This increase is reflected in a shift to the right to a new and higher demand curve, D_1. Note the relationship of points directly above and to the right of P on the new curve–points A and B, respectively. With an increase in demand, the same quantity would be demanded as before at a higher price–A compared with P–or a greater quantity would be demanded at the same price–B compared with P. (Work out for yourself the limiting adjustments in price or quantity to a decline in demand.)

But the actual adjustment probably lies somewhere between these extremes at P_1, which represents the combination of a somewhat higher price and a greater quantity demanded. Note that for the extremes to represent the final adjustments to an increase in demand, the supply schedule intersecting the two curves would have to be vertical if A were the new market price, or horizontal if B were the "new," unchanged, market price. We aren't discussing supply here, but we can't resist the opportunity to point out that a vertical supply schedule would mean that output of steak would not be increased no matter how attractive the price to suppliers, and that a horizontal schedule would indicate that output could be increased with no change in unit costs. Once we study supply, we

Figure 2.1
Increase in Demand for Steak.

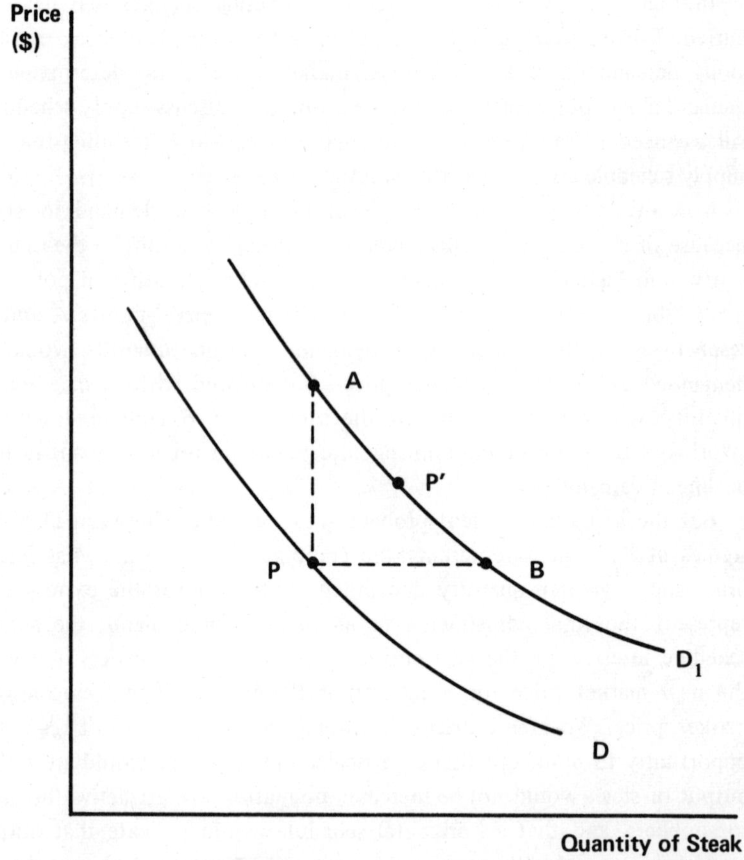

will find that the first case would be quite rare, while the latter is not too unrealistic. But here we have only tried to explain the difference in meaning between a change in demand and a change in quantity demanded.

We should not get the impression that markets adjust immediately to a change in conditions of demand or supply. In this case, after an increase in demand, the initial, immediate movement would be from P to A. But then supply would react to the higher price by expanding out towards P_1, where it would meet the demand schedule. With the expansion in supply, quantity demanded would slide down D_1 towards its meeting with the supply schedule.

Thus, while markets might be in a constant state of disequilibrium as changes occur in demand and supply schedules, what really matters in a smoothly functioning market system is that markets are also in a continual state of motion towards equilibrium in reaction to the disturbing forces.

Furthermore, our staccato-step description of the sequence of events—the equilibrium at P, the implied sudden shift of the demand schedule upwards, the much higher price for the same quantity purchased, and the expanded supply to reach a new equilibrium at a lower price than the initial reaction price to the increased demand—does not do justice to the smoothness of the market mechanism. The old saying, "nature does not make jumps," closely applies to the market system.

Income rises gradually over the years, so that there are many intermediate slight rises in the demand schedule for steak before D_1 is reached. That is, we should really draw many demand schedules between D and D_1. Consequently, supply does not adjust all at once to a sharp increase in demand, but reacts to each of the slight impulses upward in the demand schedule. On the other hand, though, supply adjustments may require a considerable length of time to work themselves out, depending on the type of product in question. The supply of steak, for example, can rise only slowly to the stimulus of increased demand. Despite great advances in animal husbandry, the steer can't change its anatomy toward its steak-producing parts, nor can the birth rate for meat producers move up suddenly.

What keeps the market system operating effectively is the fact that individual changes away from equilibrium are slight and that adjustment forces operate to try to restore equilibrium between supply and demand.

Elasticity of Demand

We have talked a great deal about important aspects of demand—the underlying determinants of demand, the demand schedule, and changes in demand—but so far we have said very little about the steepness of the *slope* of the demand schedule. Does it slope downward sharply or gently? That is, is the quantity demanded insensitive or sensitive to price changes? If it moves downward sharply, it means there is little increase in the quantity demanded if the price falls; in this case, we say that the quantity demanded for the product is insensitive to price changes. But if the demand curve falls gently, it means there is a much larger increase in the quantity demanded for the same decline in price; here, we say the quantity demanded is sensitive to price changes.

Borrowing a concept from the physical sciences, economists have developed the term *elasticity* to measure the sensitivity of quantity-demanded changes to price changes. The *elasticity of demand* is the ratio of the relative changes in quantity demanded to the relative changes in price. Note that elasticity (often represented symbolically by the Greek eta [η]) has a negative sign, because quantity and price changes move in opposite directions. Furthermore, note that the "elasticity of demand" stands for *price* elasticity of demand. We have discussed the sensitivity of other aspects of demand. For instance, we concluded that the demand for steak was highly income sensitive; thus steak has a high *income* elasticity of demand. But since our primary concern is with the quantity-price variables, "the" elasticity of demand reflects this relationship.

When the relative change in quantity demanded is greater than the relative change in price, we call the demand *elastic*. When the two relative changes are equal, we have a *unitary* elasticity of demand, or an elasticity of 1. When the relative change in quantity demanded falls short of the relative change in price—and keep in mind these elasticity types apply to price increases as well as decreases—the elasticity of demand is *inelastic*. (We tend to omit the negative sign of elasticity in discussion and call demand elastic when elasticity is greater than 1, algebraically, less than -1.)

Elasticity of demand bears a close relationship to dollar sales, called revenues, which the seller receives for his product. Revenue equals the quantity sold multiplied by the price, assuming all units are sold at the same price. Thus, when demand is elastic, and the increase in quantity sold more than compensates for the decline in price, total revenue will rise if price falls, and fall if price rises. Similarly, when unitary elasticity prevails, revenue will remain unchanged, whether prices fall or rise, since the quantity change will exactly balance out the price change in the opposite direction. Finally, if demand is inelastic, with relative quantity responses falling short of the relative price change, revenue will fall as prices decline, and rise as prices go up.

It is one thing to understand the meaning of elasticity, but it is more important to understand the conditions that will make the demand elastic for one product and inelastic for another. Fortunately, we already have the tools to explain the forces that determine the degree of elasticity of a product's demand. It's now just a matter of focusing our past analysis on the issue at hand.

We relied on substitution and income effects to explain the downward slope of the demand curve itself. Not only do these effects explain the direction of the slope of the demand curve, but their intensity also explains the steepness of the drop in the curve, and consequently its elasticity. Since income effects are usually slight, substitutability is undoubtedly the main determinant of elasticity. If the product is easily substitutable for other things—steak for other cuts of meat, assuming their prices do not change, for example—a fall in price will call forth a large increase in quantity demanded, making for an elastic curve. Similarly, the poor substitutability for necessities makes their demand schedules inelastic.

For any given product, elasticity does not tend to be a constant over a large price range. As price falls, more will be demanded; but there is no need for the ratio between the relative change in quantity demanded and the relative change in prices to remain the same. On the average, as we would gain more and more units of the product (a consequence of falling prices), the substitution effect would weaken—either because of declining marginal utility from additional units of the product itself, or because of the growth in marginal utility of the goods we forego to acquire more units of the product in question. But the income effect would expand as long as demand were elastic, because of the increasing role of the good in our budget. It is better not to predict the course of the elasticity over a price range, but rather just to acknowledge that the demand schedule's elasticity may vary for different price levels.

If elasticity had no importance in economic decisions for the household or firm, there would be little sense, to put it mildly, in explaining its meaning or its size in particular cases. But elasticity does significantly affect economic decisions and economic results.

Take the pricing policy of a firm selling in an imperfect market. If the demand for its product is elastic, then it knows that it can increase revenues by selling at a lower price. Of course, the firm must also consider the cost structure in its price-output policy, but it at least knows sales will go well if it can sell more cheaply. Then, too, elasticity can explain the need for regulating utility price and output decisions. If the demand for, say, electricity is inelastic, it would probably pay electric companies to raise prices, thereby increasing revenues (if regulating bodies did not prevent this profit-maximizing behavior).

The demand for agricultural staples is undoubtedly inelastic. This means that if farmers in general increased their output in pursuit of their own profit-maximizing interests, the market price would fall faster than the increase in quantity demanded, revenues would decline, and this method of trying to raise their own incomes would be self-defeating. Thus, inelasticity of demand for farm products explains the frequent efforts of farmers to limit individual output through collective efforts.

So much for justification of the study of elasticity. More detailed applications of the concept appear in the book on microeconomic issues in this series. So much, too, for the study of consumer demand. Let's move on to a discussion of the household's decisions on its work, or the factor supply decisions which determine how much the household will earn to make its demand effective.

Summary

Purchasing power limits household consumption, with income being the major determinant of purchasing power for any given time period. The higher our incomes, the more we buy; but the direction of our demand tends to shift away from necessities, toward luxuries. The shift is a relative one though, and there are only a small number of products for which our consumption would actually decline as income rose.

Demand for particular products at a given price depends not only on our income, but also on our taste and on the price of substitutes. The household is in consumption equilibrium—that is, maximizing its satisfaction—when the last dollar spent on all products yields equal satisfaction. When the price of the product falls, the quantity demanded will increase to restore this equilibrium. The household will be influenced by a substitution effect which induces it to buy more of the product instead of other relatively more expensive products. At the same time, an income effect will tend to reinforce this substitution effect, because the lower price will to some extent increase the household's total purchasing power and most likely direct consumption toward this product as well as toward others. For a few inferior goods, the income effect works against the substitution effect; but only for a very few would the negative income effect actually outweigh the positive substitution effect, and result in reduced quantity purchased at lower prices.

Market demand is the sum of the individual households' demand. When prices fall, not only do those households already in the market expand their purchases, but in addition new ones enter the market. Thus, for some goods—those for which the number of households is more sensitive to price change than the individual household's demand—the market demand curve is more elastic than the single household's curve.

Demand curves shift when there are changes in the fundamental determinants of demand. A rise in income, a strengthening of tastes for the product, a rise in the price of substitutes will all tend to shift demand curves upward, to the right. This means that over time either more would be demanded at the same price, or the same amount would be demanded at a higher price, or a combination of higher price and increased quantity demanded would prevail.

Elasticity of demand also greatly depends on product substitutability. Those products which can easily substitute for others in our "shopping list" will have a high elasticity of demand, so that total dollar purchases (revenue to the selling firms) will rise as price falls, since the relative increase in quantity demanded will rise more than the relative decline in price.

Chapter Three The Household as Supplier of Labor

There is much sound economics in the biblical dictum, "By the sweat of our brow we shall earn our daily bread." All that demand we spoke about in the last chapter requires income; and for most of us, income comes from work, which takes time and effort. We've come a long way since Bible days in reducing the effort aspect of work. Today, manpower requires much less horsepower than in the "good old days." In fact, "sweat" has become an unpopular word, describing a condition to be avoided, except perhaps in conjunction with our free-time activities. The ads tell us we are socially, if not morally, obligated to prevent or neutralize sweat by using the current antiperspirant and/or deodorant.

But no matter how much we lighten work, even if we exalt it less, it still takes time—time we would rather spend doing something else. It is this time cost of work that limits the amount of time we are willing to work, and consequently limits our income and demand. Income is desirable, but the goal of the individual worker in maximizing his total economic satisfaction is not to maximize his income. If it were, he could achieve this goal by the simple practice of working 168 hours a week. This is a practice simple to formulate, impossible to achieve.

Thus, the worker does not want to maximize his income through unlimited application of work time and effort. What then does he try to maximize? How much labor does he want to offer on the market during a certain time period or, in economics language, what is his equilibrium labor supply per time period?

We approach the answer to these similar questions by noting that like all economic behavior this decision requires a choice among alternatives. On the one hand, the worker wants income from work, because this income allows him to buy the goods and services he wants to consume. On the other hand, the worker wants free time, time away from work. We are practically born with the knowledge that these goals conflict, in that our income depends on the amount of free time we are willing to forego to devote to work. In short, then, the worker seeks his optimum combination of earnings and free time, knowing that he can only increase one by reducing the other.

Our Various Uses of Time

Since time is the chief factor in our work decisions, it is fitting that we discuss the various uses of time and, more specifically, the assumptions and classifications of time our analysis of labor supply uses. We have already implied the crudest assumption regarding our attitudes toward time. As a first step in the analysis, the economist assumes that all work time is undesirable and all free time is pleasurable. If this sounds to you like an application of the 19th century utilitarian philosophy of pleasure and pain, you are on the right track. This classification of time, now some 150 years old, stems directly from that thinking. We know the assumption is unrealistic, in that many people derive some pleasure from their work and that there are a lot of things we do during our free time which we find more painful than work. A visit to the dentist hardly comes under the heading of fun and games. We will relax this assumption later on in the chapter; but at this stage, it will help our understanding if we follow a weakened form of the assumption—i.e., that, on balance, time spent away from the job is more satisfying than time spent on the job.

To show the age of this simplified classification of time, economists call the two classes of time "work time" and "leisure." Now, Webster tells us that leisure is time devoted to rest, relaxation, and contemplation. How much of the average modern American's nonwork time is devoted to these pursuits? Most of us pursue our leisure with an energy and effort that raises the sweat the Bible tells us should come from work. But this change in taste doesn't bother our analysis. All we need assume is that we derive satisfaction from our free-time pursuits, no matter how frantic the chase would seem to a 19th century utilitarian. After all, it is our choice.

The opportunity cost of the time spent in leisure is the earnings foregone from time spent at work. But within our choice of a leisure-time activity itself, there is an opportunity cost in the opportunity foregone to engage in some other leisure-time activity. We can look upon leisure as a consumption good. The cost of an hour's leisure is an hour's income. But to look at the choice of our use of leisure hours, we must consider both the time cost of not doing something else and the money cost of the activity we choose.

If we have 50 hours a week for leisure—let's ignore the time required for sleep, eating, etc., for the moment—how we will use it depends on our tastes and on our purchasing power. Given the amount of money we have to spend on leisure activities, we follow the decision process described in the last chapter, but with some modification. We still maximize our total satisfaction by equalizing the satisfaction gained from the last dollar spent on each activity. But we realize now that the time cost of consuming leisure plays a part in determining our tastes in and our choice of leisure activities.

For example, we might get a lot of fun out of playing golf; but a game on a crowded public course may take four or five hours. We derive pleasure from hitting the ball, from the companionship experienced during the game, and perhaps from the 19th hole; but it is a person with unusual preferences who enjoys waiting an hour before teeing off or tracking down a misfired shot in the wilderness politely known as the rough. We could cut two hours off the game by playing on a less crowded (probably private) course, using a caddy and a golf cart; these are two hours which we can consider waste, or nonpleasurable, or even (like work) painful time. But this reduction in unwanted time takes money. The person with a lot of money to spend on leisure will find that it pays to incur these costs.

We can squeeze out the two unwanted hours, and use that time on other leisure activities that yield pleasure. The marginal satisfaction of the last golfing hour, say the third, has risen, but so has the cost. Still, the high-income player can now do many other things with his saved time—things which equalize the marginal satisfaction from the last dollar spent on them with that spent on golf.

The low-income golfer might have the same preferences, finding the same aspects of a slow game equally distasteful. Similarly, he might raise his marginal satisfaction from the third hour on the course just as much by incurring the costs to eliminate the unwanted hours. But if he did so, he would find he would have little money left for other leisure activities. He would not be able to bring the marginal satisfaction from the last dollar spent on them to the last dollar spent on golf. He would be in consumption disequilibrium. Acting rationally, he takes the bitter time with the sweet in playing golf; though he derives less marginal satisfaction from the last hour on the game than the high-income player, he now has enough money left to spend on other leisure goods and services so as to equate the marginal satisfaction from the last dollar spent on everything.

The lower our income, the less we will spend on our leisure. The less we have to spend in total, the less we will tend to spend on any one thing. If we have next to no money to spend on leisure, we will spend a lot of time watching television, engaging in conversation, and waiting for the leisure goods and services we do manage to buy. Talk is cheap if you have no money to spend on other uses of your time. Poets have written about the simple tastes of the poor. The hard-headed economist observes that it is not their tastes that are meager, just their income.

The nature of leisure time makes the difference between household and individual labor supply significantly different. While consumption expenditures can be pooled, leisure cannot be shared. If the husband worked an extra hour, it might mean a much bigger addition to household income than if the wife were to contibute an extra hour. But if he is already working a full schedule and she only a few hours, if any at all, it might represent a rational household decision for her to be the one to work more, considering individual time-income preferences. She cannot sit home and take his leisure for him.

Income-Leisure Preference and Equilibrium Labor Supply

Following the method used in deriving the individual demand curve for a product, we will begin to study the labor supply schedule by determining the equilibrium work effort at a given price–in this case, wage rate. After deriving the labor supply schedule for the individual, we will move on to the market supply schedule, and then to the supply schedule for individual households.

Let us start by assuming that at an hourly wage of $3.00 the worker in question is at his equilibrium labor supply when working 40 hours per week to earn $120. What does this mean? It means that the worker has matched his subjective valuation of an extra hour's leisure with the market's valuation of the worth of an extra hour of his work time, expressed by his hourly wage rate.

He works the 40th hour because he can earn $3.00 from this effort. Presumably, if he didn't work, the personal value of the 129th hour away from the job would yield him less satisfaction than $3.00 would buy. Expressed differently, the price of leisure, $3.00, is more than he cares to pay for an additional unit (hour) of it.

Now, if he is at equilibrium at the 40th hour, he will not be willing to work 41 hours. If he still only gets $3.00 for the extra hour of work, he will decide against offering it, because now the 128th hour off the job is worth more to him than $3.00. That is, at the margin of the 41st hour, the hour of leisure would yield more satisfaction than he could gain by exchanging it for the income from an hour's extra work.

Again, as in the case of demand, we don't have to speak of declining marginal utilities of leisure or income to explain why the more we have of one, the more of it we are willing to give up in exchange for an extra unit of the other. All we need assume is that the relationship between the marginal utilities turns in favor of the "product" that has become scarcer to us.

Although the individual worker would not choose to work an hour beyond his equilibrium labor input at the going wage, he would assuredly accept the opportunity to work more if he were offered overtime pay for the extra hours. If the overtime rate were 50 percent above his base pay, he would receive $4.50 for each extra hour of work. This would be too good an opportunity for him to pass up. Expressed in more formal economic language, the amount of utility he would receive from an extra hour's labor would exceed the utility of the leisure foregone to contribute that labor effort. In other words, the utility that could be derived from \$4.50 exceeds the utility of the foregone leisure, which is valued at something a little more than \$3.00 for the 128th hour—only a little more, because "nature does not make jumps."

In the real world, however, most workers may have a subjective labor supply curve, but they are not able to regulate their hours of work by small gradations of time. For most jobs, they must be willing to work the set schedule if they are to work at all. This explains why some workers actually refuse overtime, given the option to do so. Many workers, especially older men, work more hours than they care to at the going wage. They choose to work, not because they can reach an equilibrium position between income and leisure, because they cannot, but because they prefer work to their only alternative under the circumstances, which is not to work at all. They might value their last hour of leisure at a very high rate, say at \$5.00 an hour. Therefore, they would not be attracted to more work by the overtime rate of \$4.50. It is only because they are at a disequilibrium in their income-leisure combination at the fixed schedule that they refuse overtime.

The opposite group at a disequilibrium position contains those who value their marginal hour of leisure at less than the wage rate. These workers, characteristically those with pressing consumption needs and wants who head households having growing children, would like to work longer hours at the going wage than their set schedules provide. Of course, they would be very happy to work overtime. But in the absence of overtime opportunities, they would seek extra hours of work on another job. Moonlighters, as a class, are those who are at a disequilibrium in their income-leisure position on their first job, in that they would be willing to trade their last, and perhaps, additional hours of leisure which they value at something less than \$3.00 an hour for work hours and the extra income they bring.

Individual Labor Supply Schedule

So far we have established a point on the workers' labor supply curve which relates the amount of time he would offer to the labor market for the wage, or hourly income, he would receive from his work. Following the method of developing product demand, we will proceed to study the worker's reaction to wage changes. We will again speak of substitution and income effects, but we will find that the relationship between these effects and the worker's labor supply differs radically from the pattern for product demand.

Substitution Effect

Let's assume that the wage rate rises to $4.00 an hour. We will think in terms of the demand for leisure, which is the counterpart of the supply of labor. Now the price of leisure has gone up, making each hour more expensive. Here leisure is no different from any other product. With a rise in its price, there will be a tendency to substitute other goods and services for leisure. We give up leisure to acquire them; or, in other words, the substitution effect of a wage increase reduces the quantity of leisure demanded, and thereby increases the supply of labor.

Income Effect

The big difference between the demand for leisure and the demand for any other product arises from the income effect. That leisure has become more expensive does not reduce our purchasing power, as would be the case with other products; on the contrary, it increases our spending power, and substantially so. Keep in mind that the price of leisure, by the hour, is nothing else but the wage rate. The rise to $4.00 from $3.00 an hour increases our income by 1/3; or, assuming we work a 40-hour week, it raises our weekly income from $120 to $160.

Now, if leisure is a normal good (and there is really no reason to believe otherwise), the income effect on the demand for leisure from a wage increase would be positive, and strongly so. That is, the income effect of a wage increase would act to reduce the supply of labor.

Thus, unlike the pattern for product demand, the substitution and income effects from a wage change work with opposing forces. The former affects the quantity of leisure demanded in the opposite direction of the wage change, the latter in the same direction. When the price of the usual product falls, the consumer tends to buy it both because it is now more attractive to buy than substitutes and because of a slight additional stimulant to consumption since his real purchasing power has increased as a result of the price decline in one of his budget items. When the price of leisure rises, he is induced to buy less leisure (supply more labor) because leisure has become more expensive than other "products"; but this force to "buy" less is opposed by a strong force inducing him to "buy" more leisure (supply less labor) because the rise in leisure's price has so substantially raised his purchasing power.

Consequently, the actual direction of the worker's quantity of labor supplied in response to a wage increase depends on the relative strength of the income and substitution effects. If the former dominates, the labor supply will fall. If the latter dominates, the labor supply will rise.

It is impossible to tell in advance the nature of the individual's labor supply schedule—i.e., whether it is positively sloped with the hours of work offered to the market rising with wages, or negatively sloped, with the hours of work supplied moving inversely to the wage rate. But if we know something about the individual's income-leisure preference, we might correctly predict the direction of his supply curve.

For example, many students who work their way through school have a negatively sloped curve. Their income needs are more or less fixed. They want to make enough money to pay their school costs and basic living expenses. Since their education will prepare them for higher earnings in later life, their school expenses are to be considered largely an investment in future earning power. Working at the same time they attend school is not only a hardship, but, in addition, too much market work may weaken their investment by reducing their school efficiency. For these students, a rise in their market wage rate will probably have a strong income effect on their demand for "leisure." Thus, the higher the wage, the more likely the student would be to reduce his market labor effort. To broaden the analysis, anyone with fixed income goals would tend to reduce his work effort, the higher his wage.

On the other hand, when income goals are vague, and the worker is striving to reach a higher economic, and perhaps social, status, his supply schedule would tend to be positively sloped, with the substitution effect of the wage increase on the demand for leisure outweighing the income effect. After graduation, marriage, and the arrival of children, the former student would probably experience a drastic shift in his labor supply schedule. Now, his income goals would no longer be fixed, and he would probably offer more labor, the higher his wage.

Apart from the stimulation to labor supply of vague consumption goods associated with the postschool years, the worker would find he would have less to lose in foregoing other uses of time to invest in his skills, once his formal schooling were completed. Thus, both his changing consumption needs and the relaxed pressures of alternative economically productive uses of his time would act to make his labor supply schedule positively sloped. Hours of work offered would move in step with wages.

Not only does the labor supply schedule change for the same worker during different periods of his life, but, in addition, the direction of the curve may change under moment-in-time schedule conditions for different wage levels. Textbooks often depict the typical labor supply schedule with a backward bend to it. First, labor supply increases with wages. Then, at a relatively high wage level, the curve bends. At a still higher wage level, less labor is offered. Of course, the bend would occur at varying wage levels for different workers. Figure 3.1 presents such a labor supply schedule.

There is much logic to this description of the individual labor supply schedule. The lowest wage on the curve is at the subsistence level. Minimum-wage legislation and welfare programs either prevent or discourage labor supply at lower wages. The opportunity to rise up the socioeconomic scale at wages moving above this level outweighs the positive income effect of higher earnings on the demand for leisure, and results in a positively sloped supply schedule over the lower part of the wage range.

But as wages rise and work time increases and leisure time shrinks, the marginal utility of an extra hour's leisure rises relative to that of the income from an extra hour's work. The income effect then increases relative to the substitution effect, and, at wages above *A* on Figure 3.1, outweighs it. Thus, in the higher section of the wage range, the labor supply schedule is negatively sloped with the worker taking the gain from a wage increase partly in the form of shorter hours.

Compare the two points *B* and *B′* on our hypothetical worker's labor supply curve. Hours of work supplied are the same, although the wage rate is much higher at *B′* than *B*. If the wage is $2.00 an hour at *B* and $5.00 an hour at *B′*, and if both points measure 40-hour schedules, the curve tells us that the worker is at an equilibrium position in his income-leisure decision in this schedule when the wage is either $2.00 an hour or $5.00 per hour. Expressed differently, he values the leisure hour foregone to work the 40th hour at either $2.00 or $5.00. How is this possible?

This paradox is resolved when we note that he is at quite different weekly income levels at the two wages—$80 at *B* and $200 at *B′*. At the lower wage, he values his last hour of leisure cheaply because he has a

Figure 3.1
Backward-Bending Labor Supply Schedule.

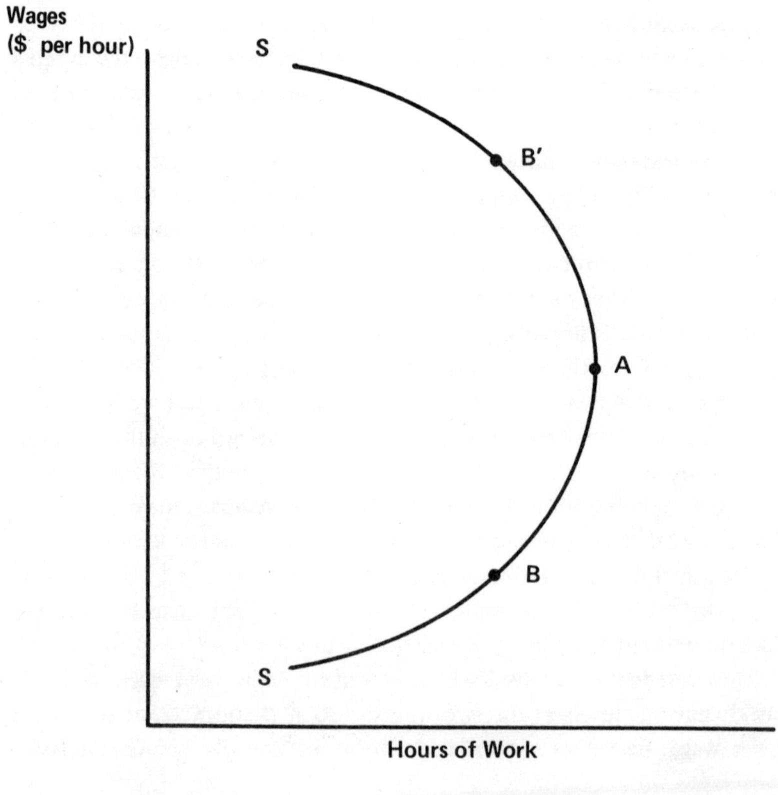

pressing need for money income. His low valuation of his leisure at the lower wage is not based on an intrinsically weak desire for leisure, but on the fact that at this low income he can't afford to trade leisure for income except at a low price for leisure. On the other hand, with an income of $200 a week he is in a position to satisfy his tastes for leisure, and is willing to pay $5 an hour in foregone earnings for it at the margin.

Let's not get confused about the meaning of equilibrium. Economic analysis really does not try to distort reality, although at times it may seem to do so. The worker is certainly better off at wage B' than at wage B, and it is a much preferred position. But he doesn't set his own wages. Equilibrium simply implies that he gets to his best income-leisure position *under the circumstances*. The circumstances are much worse for him at a lower wage rate, but the supply schedule merely attempts to report his various equilibrium positions at every wage.

Analogy of Labor Supply with Supply of Savings

The household not only supplies labor to firms, but it also supplies its savings in return for interest or dividend income. We are focusing only on labor markets in this book, but let's just take a look at the decision on savings, mainly to show the close analogy between this decision and the labor supply one.

As with the supply of labor, the supplier of loan funds makes a choice between earnings based on sacrifice and the benefits of an alternative which reduces earnings. For labor supply, the sacrifice is of leisure time for earnings; for supply of loan funds, the sacrifice is of current consumption potential for future earnings. The interest rate plays the role of the wage rate.

At higher interest rates, the lender faces both a substitution and income effect. The former makes him lend more in that he can now gain a greater amount of future income by increasing his savings. But the income effect makes him save less in that his total purchasing power, present and future, rises with the rate of interest. He can afford to "buy" more current consumption. Which effect dominates? Again there is uncertainty because the forces of the two effects oppose each other. If the saver has fixed future consumption goals, or if he is saving for a particular fixed purchase—say, education of his children or even a given total bundle of goods which would represent a desired standard of living in later life—then the income effect on the demand for current consumption would dominate the substitution effect, and the individual would save less at higher rates of interest.

The supply curve of loan funds would probably look very much like that of the supply schedule of labor; it would rise over the lower range of the interest rate, then bend backward and finally fall with higher rates of interest. The interest rate would be on the Y-axis of Figure 3.1, and the dollar amount of savings per time period would be measured along the X-axis.

Market Supply Schedule of Labor

Just as was the case in extending the individual consumer demand for a particular product to the whole market, so too the market supply schedule of labor of a particular class or occupation would be influenced both by changes in the supply of those already in the market and by entrances to and departures from the market.

The big difference between the build-up of the two market curves comes from the uncertain patterns of the individual response to a wage change. For product demand, a drop in price would both increase the quantity demanded by those already in the market and swell the total demand by the addition of new entrants to the market.

But for labor supply, a rise in wages (at least to high levels) would probably reduce the labor supply of those already in the market. However, the backward bend to the individual supply curve would tend to be straightened out by the response to higher wages of those not originally in the market. Retired people and others not in the labor force would be lured to the market by the earnings opportunity of higher wages. In the long run, workers would acquire the needed skills to enter the now high-wage field. Thus, the effect of higher wages on workers not currently in the market would be similar to the influence of lower product price on potential consumers; the effect in both cases would be to increase market participation—on the supply side for labor and on the demand side for goods.

For labor supply, then, the market supply schedule would tend to have a positive slope over a much wider wage range than the individual supply schedule; in fact, it might never bend backward over the entire realistic wage range. This tendency would be more pronounced in the long run than in the short run. Again, analysis checks with reality, in that fields with rising wages experience a growth in total labor supply. Stated more clearly for market purposes, an increase in demand for labor of a particular type, as expressed by a tendency for the wage to rise, would be joined by an accommodating increase in quantity supplied. Thus, labor markets function as we expect markets to, despite the peculiarity of the individual labor supply schedule.

Household Labor Supply: Working Wives

We have already noted that extension of individual labor supply to that of the household as a unit involves complications that do not arise when we contrast household with individual consumer demand. The difficulty arises because of the inability to share leisure time. (Don't be confused by the popular meaning of the word "share," which is often used loosely to apply to doing things together. Husband and wife may take their own leisure together, but they can't divide up their hours off the job.)

The general pattern in a family unit is for the husband definitely to work, and for the wife to make a close decision as to whether to work or not.

Women's Liberation tells us that this system is all wrong. If the income from one adult would suffice to meet household consumption goals, then the spouse who could earn the most should work and the other should stay home to manage the household. Women have the same native ability as men, and more and more they are gaining equal training and education; therefore, if employment discrimination were eliminated, the decision as to who would be the principal breadwinner would vary from household to household, with earning power being the main factor in the decision. Then the marginal decision of whether to work or not would apply to either spouse, not just to the woman.

But this is no place to get into a discussion of what should be. Our task is to describe the factors that explain the actual situation. The facts of the matter are that almost all married men work, or at least seek work, while only some women do. For example, almost 100 percent of married men 25-34 years old are in the labor force. The percentage of working wives of the same age is only about 40 percent.

The main reason wives do not seek gainful employment is that their time and effort is required at home. However, their participation in the work force has been increasing in recent years. Various good reasons have been offered to explain this trend–higher household consumption goals; better and longer education and training for women; change in composition of job requirements away from factory to office, away from heavy to lighter physical effort; and growing social acceptance of the wife's working. But despite all these forces, wives still stay home in droves.

The strength of the need to perform home duties not only depends on the tastes of the individual household, or wife, but also on the income of the principal breadwinner. Like any other economically rational decision-maker, the wife tries to maximize the satisfaction, or utility, from the various uses of her time. She would contribute an hour to the labor market if the earnings from this hour at least compensated for the loss of an hour's time doing something else. The higher her husband's income, the less would be the marginal returns from this extra income relative to the utility sacrificed by giving up the hour to work. Thus, the wife of the high-income husband is less likely to work than the wife of the low-income husband. Again, both wives may have the same intrinsic subjective valuation of the marginal hour off the job; but for the high-income wife, the gain from giving up the hour off the job would be less than for the low-income wife.

To derive the labor supply schedule for the typical wife, it is helpful to introduce still another concept of time. Along with market work time (which is considered painful) and leisure time (which is pleasurable), there is a third class of time, which we can call nonmarket work time. This consists of the time used by the wife to perform household duties. When the wife shops, cleans, etc., she performs useful services; hence, the time so spent is considered work. But it is nonmarket work, since she doesn't receive an income for the services.

Let's assume that this type of work is just as "painful" as market work, but is essential to the maintenance of the household. Under this arbitrary assumption, if she could find substitutes for the house services, she would engage in market work–provided the earnings from her paid work exceeded the cost of the substitutes. Cost is clearly involved in using other means than her own labor to perform these home duties. Appliances, frozen and prepared foods, babysitters, and other servants can get the job done, but often at a substantial expense.

The higher the wife's earning power, the more likely it is that she will find it economical to purchase these services. Therefore, the labor supply schedule for wives is more apt to be positively sloped over a realistic wage range than that of her husband. She doesn't have to reduce her leisure in order to work more at higher wages, but can cut into the third use of time by reducing her time and effort in housework. Don't forget that as her wage rises, it becomes increasingly easier financially to employ other means of performing housework.

Consequently, a wife could increase her market work time and also her leisure by drastically reducing her home effort. It is quite likely that many wives today work less and have more leisure time than their mother, even though they work much more in the labor market.

How can you explain the fact that many wives lose money by working—i.e., the cost of substitutes for their labor at home exceeds their market earnings? Economic analysis has an answer for every financial practice that might at first view seem irrational. All we must do is drop our assumption that both types of work, market and home, are equally painful. In this case, the wife suffers less pain—or may even derive some pleasure—from market work. In effect, the household is making a consumption expense by her working. They are buying a subtle form of utility by reducing the total disutility associated with work.

By dropping the assumption of equal pain for both types of work, we can also explain the opposite situation—the case of the wife who refuses market work, even if home work substitutes are cheaper than her earnings. Suppose small children are present. The wife, or perhaps both spouses, consider her care of the children less painful than market work, which would yield higher earnings than the cost of a babysitter. Or, she might consider that her superior contribution to the upbringing of the children is worth more than the differential of her earnings over the sitter's wages. In either case, she would be less likely to work at a given wage than a wife in a household without children. Thus, the data which show substantially less labor force participation by wives with small children than other wives either reflect the high cost of babysitters or the high valuation put on time spent by the wife on child care.

Maintenance Time

There is still a fourth class of time to go along with leisure, market work, and nonmarket work time. This is the time required to maintain the human machine, and is principally composed of the hours required for eating and sleeping. Two-hour lunches have very little to do with maintenance. Rarely is such a long period devoted to eating that is carried out alone. When a meal is eaten with friends, all but a few minutes can be considered leisure time. When it is eaten with business associates or contacts, most of the time can be considered work time; in fact the incidence of stomach ulcers among executives suggests that not enough time or application is devoted to satisfying the maintenance requirements of eating.

Let's move to sleep. On the average, close to one-third of our lives is spent sleeping. There's little one can do to cut down on this time. Some people can go long periods with little sleep, but nature has a way of catching up with those who burn the candle at both ends.

Suppose a "sleep" pill were invented, one that would strengthen the restorative powers of sleep so that we only needed two hours of sleep a night. Why not envision such a pill? We have pills for almost everything else. Let's further assume that the cost of the pill was negligible.

Most of us would be very eager to take advantage of this pill. By cutting into this maintenance time, which lies in a limbo of nothingness between the pain of work and the pleasure of leisure, we could increase both our income from extra time at work and our leisure.

Who would refuse the pill? Those unfortunates who preferred oblivion to the reality of life. Besides the sick, the poor and the unhappy sleep a great deal—the poor because they have no opportunity for extra earnings and have probably already reached zero marginal utility from their leisure time; the unhappy because a neutral hour of nothingness provides more net satisfaction—zero—than the disutility of another hour of wakeful misery.

Labor Supply and Occupational Choice

Up to now, we have just been talking about labor supply in general, without specifying what jobs we choose for our life's work. Many workers follow more than one occupation during their lifetime, but most stick mainly to the same field. Of course, switching jobs is common, but we are talking about classifiable occupations.

If the labor market were perfectly competitive, if we all had the same ability, and if tastes for different types of work were uniformly distributed, earnings *within* each occupation would be the same. Differences in pay *among* occupations would reflect differences in costs required to obtain the skills used in performing the duties of the particular occupations followed.

For example, assume there are only two occupations, typist and pharmacist. The pharmacist makes more money, but the training required to become a pharmacist costs much more than that required to become a typist. Under the assumption stated, if income got out of line so that the earnings of the pharmacists exceeded those of the typists by more than the extra costs of training and education, workers would begin switching from typing to pharmacy.

But, of course, the real world does not witness such a smooth functioning of labor markets. Why? Because most of us are ignorant of precise earnings differences; different occupations have different levels of prestige and popularity; we differ in ability; and we have different opportunities to acquire the training and education needed to perform the duties of high-paying occupations.

As individuals, we may select our occupation on a hit-or-miss basis; but it still pays us to follow occupations for which we have interest and aptitude, provided there is a market for our acquired skills. Then we are most apt to derive the highest benefits, economic and psychological, from our occupation.

Why then do so many people "choose" routine, low-paying jobs? These are the jobs which take little training or education costs to fill. Undoubtedly, there are many people who are unable to learn and acquire the skills associated with jobs which need a great deal of education. But probably the greatest reason for many people's low position in the income scale is their lack of opportunity to undertake the costly and time-consuming process of education. We have expanded aid to those undertaking education, but we are still far short of providing equality of opportunity financially. Evidence of this malfunctioning of the market system is the fact that the earnings of the highly educated and trained more than compensate for the cost of the training. Some of this potential market earnings difference is suppressed by social legislation and custom, which arbitrarily raises the wages of the untrained and unskilled. But, then, the market disequilibrium takes the form of greater unemployment among these less skilled groups.

Summary

As with all economic decisions, the equilibrium income-leisure position for the individual represents a maximizing situation. In the case of labor supply, the worker is maximizing his total utility from his combination of earnings and leisure. Since earnings take labor time and effort, the decision comes down to the optimum choice of distribution of time between work and leisure. This optimum is reached when the marginal utility of an hour's time off the job just equals the marginal utility of the earnings of an extra hour's labor.

Unlike the case for product demand, the direction a change in individual labor supply will take in reaction to a change in wages is uncertain, with the uncertainty arising from the conflict in substitution and income effects. If the wage rate increases, the substitution effect encourages an increase in hours of work supplied, or a reduction in hours of leisure, because the price of leisure has risen. Leisure now tends to be substituted for by other relatively cheaper "goods." On the other hand, the income effect acts to reduce the supply of labor, since with a wage increase the worker's income rises, leading him to "buy" more leisure and other normal "goods."

The direction of labor supply depends on the relative strength of the two effects. If consumption goals are more or less fixed, the income effect will dominate, and labor supply will fall. If goals are vague and the worker is striving to reach a higher socioeconomic class, the substitution effect will prevail, and labor supply will rise with the wage rate.

The conventional description of the typical individual labor supply curve has it sloping upwards positively over the lower part of the relevant wage range—that is, with the labor supply rising with the wage rate. Then, the curve bends and slopes negatively, with the labor supply falling over the high-wage segment as the worker chooses to increase his leisure time from the lower level to which it had fallen while his work time was increasing.

The market labor supply schedule consists of the summation of individual labor supply curves. Since new entrants to the labor force appear at higher wages, the backward portion of the individual curves is straightened out by supply increases from this source. Consequently, the market labor schedule will be positively sloped over a wider wage range than will the individual curves.

The household labor supply includes the work effort of secondary workers, primarily the wife, as well as that of the chief breadwinner. Wives spend a great deal of time in nonmarket labor as they manage the household. In effect, then, they have three potential classes of time—market work, nonmarket work, and leisure. A rise in wages allows the purchase of costly substitutes for the wife's housework duties. If her subjective attitude towards the market and housework are the same, she will substitute other services for her own housework effort as long as the earnings from market work exceed the cost of these substitutes.

Thus, the labor supply schedule for the typical wife is more likely to be positively sloped than that of her husband; she can increase her market work effort and earnings without reducing her leisure time (in fact, she might increase it). The wife is less likely to work when there are small children in the household, because in this case the hours of home-work time do not tend to be as subjectively "painful" as hours of market work. Put less formally, the household sees positive benefits in the mother's contribution to child care.

Chapter Four The Firm as Supplier of Product

Firms are in business to make money. This statement may seem hard, cynical, and very commercial. Firms *produce* shoes and steel and hospital supplies and travel advice and literally millions of other products; but unless they can show profits to their owners after paying taxes, wages, rents, and interest costs, they will no longer continue in production. The ultimate goal of economic activity is consumption, and if a production unit cannot contribute to the purchasing power of those involved in the firm either as owners or suppliers of goods and services, it will not survive.

In this study, with the addition of a few qualifying assumptions, it can be easily seen that the individual firm's economic goal is to maximize profits. For the worker, the supply of labor to earn income for consumption takes time and effort; and to earn more income takes more effort. But for the firm, the managers responsible for running the business do not have to work harder or longer to earn higher profits. In fact, if worry and concern are elements of effort, they may even "work" less as profits expand.

Consequently, if profits are desirable, and if it takes no more of management's effort to raise profits (it is hard to see how management works any harder when the firm produces 500 units a week than when it produces 200 units), the firm will strive to maximize profits. Apart from the realistic assumption that management's effort is not related to the level of output and profits, we are also implying that the firm does not have other goals that conflict with profit maximization. Some firms in sensitive industries–steel producers, for example–are concerned about the possibility of government interference in their pricing policies; so they probably charge less than profit-maximizing prices to avoid this intervention. Other firms may fear antitrust litigation and accordingly keep their prices and profits lower than what could be attained from operation of the market system. But, in the main, we do little violence to reality in assuming that firms strive to maximize profits. Our analysis will be based on this assumption.

Profits are the difference between revenues from sales and costs of production. Thus to maximize profits, the firm will try to produce at the output level which maximizes this difference. Whatever output it decides upon in keeping with this policy will be produced by the least expensive means possible. The least-cost method depends on the relative prices and productivities of the different factors of production. Study of the decision for use of the various factors constitutes the next chapter. Here we will just assume least-cost production, and will examine the cost and revenue position of the firm to analyze the firm's output position. We begin with a discussion of costs, then go on to revenues and profits.

Fixed Costs

Costs of production are put into two classes: fixed and variable. *Fixed costs* are those which are incurred regardless of the volume of output, within limits. Costs of plant–fixtures, basic equipment, and office furniture, for example–and management are fixed; that is, they are unrelated to output. Machinery occupies a half-way position between fixed and variable costs. The initial cost of the machine is fixed; and so, too, its obsolescence and much of its depreciation are unrelated to the volume of production. But, certainly, maintenance and repair machinery costs will rise at higher levels of output.

Furthermore, machinery exemplifies the short-run nature of fixed costs. The costs incurred for a machine are sunk; and apart from resale or scrap value, these costs are the same no matter how intensively the machine is used. If business is bad, though, worn-out machines will not be replaced. Thus for any particular machine, or its replacement, the cost can vary after a time. Total annual machinery costs are therefore variable in that additions can be made if production so warrants, or not made if future sales look gloomy.

If we consider a long enough time period, all costs are variable. If current profits are low or negative, and future prospects just as bad, the firm might go out of business entirely, in the process reducing all costs to, zero. Before that, though, it can cut down on some of its overhead expenses, and even rent out space in its plant.

Fixed costs not only have a time element, but are also related to what is called the *scale of operations*. Scale differs from output in that it signifies the size of basic operations—or, if you will, fixed costs—which are fundamental to production.

Recall that we defined fixed costs as unrelated to output, *within limits*. Suppose the firm is successful; after increasing output, it finds further growth in production can not be feasibly made without expanding the plant. By infeasibility at present scale, we mean that unit costs could be reduced with a larger plant. If the firm feels sales will continue at higher levels in the future, it will enlarge its plant, or perhaps build a new or second one, thereby expanding its sale of operation.

To show the scale effects of fixed costs, consider the simple example of the company medical department. Suppose it consists originally of a single nurse. Her salary is a fixed cost, and she is probably classified under overhead labor. Now, suppose output grows so much that employment triples. The firm will find its medical "staff" inadequate. Its larger labor force now requires a bureaucratized system of health standards. An X-ray machine is bought, a technician is hired, perhaps a part-time doctor is employed. The firm is unlikely to go so far as to establish a hospital on the premises, but it has expanded its fixed costs at a higher scale of operation. This specific fixed-cost medical department forms part of the scale that includes all expenses which are fixed within a sizable range of output, but which can vary over different ranges.

Scale can be reduced, too. If, for example, output and employment slackened, the nurse could be put on a part-time basis, then let go.

Since total fixed costs do not vary with output, *average fixed costs*, or cost per unit of output, obviously fall with output. In symbols, $AFC = TFC/O$. Here AFC stands for average fixed costs, TFC for total fixed costs, and O for output. From this equation, it is easy to see that an increase in output will lead to a fall in unit fixed costs.

If fixed costs were the only production costs, and if the firm could sell its output at the same price no matter at what level of production (recall from the first chapter that this is a condition of perfect competition), the firm would increase its output without limit. But all costs are not fixed. It's pretty hard to produce anything at all without workers and materials, and expenses for these productive factors constitute variable costs. We will confine our discussion of variable costs to labor costs.

Variable Costs

These are the costs which increase with output. To produce more goods requires more workers; and if we consider labor as the only variable cost, the total variable cost equals the wage bill. In symbols, $TVC = W \cdot L$, with W standing for the hourly wage rate, and L standing for the amount of labor used or, specifically, the number of man-hours employed.

We are not concerned about differences in labor types or occupations here, but are considering labor a homogeneous factor with all workers having the same efficiency and no change being made in the wage rage regardless of the number of people the firm employs. The equation shows the simple relationship of total variable costs rising because L increases with output.

But more important than the mere fact that total variable costs rise is the path which this increase takes as more and more labor is used. Variable costs are related to the productivity of the work force. Productivity is measured by output per-man-hour. In symbols, $AP = O/L$, with AP standing for average product or productivity. At low levels of output, with only a few workers utilized along with the fixed factors, the workers would be inefficiently employed. They would have to perform too many different tasks to be uniformly proficient in them.

With increased output, the workers would perform the specialized tasks which most closely fit their training and aptitudes. Output per-man-hour, or AP, would rise; and while total variable costs would increase, average variable costs, or variable costs per unit of output, would fall. Let's examine the relationship between average productivity and average variable costs in symbols. To repeat,

$$AP = \frac{O}{L} \tag{1}$$

and

$$TVC = W \cdot L \tag{2}$$

Then, from equation (2)

$$AVC = \frac{W \cdot L}{O} \tag{3}$$

AVC, average variable costs, simply means the variable costs per unit of output. Now, L/O, or manpower required per unit of output, is simply the reciprocal of O/L, output per-man-hour. Thus,

$$AVC = W/AP \tag{4}$$

To return to our analysis, output and employment rise from very low levels, AP rises, and from equation (4), average variable cost falls as a consequence of the more efficient use of labor.

But with fixed costs and scale of operations held constant, eventually the contribution of additional workers to total output falls, as each one works with less and less of the supporting capital and other fixed factors. At some level of input of labor, average product starts to fall. This is the point of *diminishing average returns*. From equation (4), we see that average variable costs start to rise beyond the level of labor input and output, at which point diminishing average returns set in.

Thus the typical pattern of average variable costs is to fall over low levels of output, and then to rise for higher levels, with the scale of operations fixed. Recall that average fixed costs decline with increases in output for all levels of output. Then, average total costs—ATC, which equals $AFC + AVC$—fall over an output range greater than that for the decline of AVC because of the depressing influence on unit costs of the continued decline in AFC. But eventually ATC also rises, because the increasing influence of diminishing returns more than outweighs the slight reducing influence on total unit costs of declining *AFC* at high levels of output.

Marginal Costs

We have already met the concept of marginal value in the discussion of utility and demand. Marginal refers to the added contribution of the last unit. *Marginal product* is the addition to total product resulting from the employment of the last worker. Note that this definition does not imply anything about the efficiency of the last worker. In fact, we assume that all workers of the same class or occupation receive the same pay and are of equal efficiency. Thus, the output attributable to the last worker depends on the effect on production of using one more unit of the same type of labor, with other factors fixed.

From the previous explanation of the effect of additional variable units on the productive efficiency of each, we learn that marginal product will rise from the addition of the first units of labor; but after a certain work force is used, *diminishing marginal returns* will set in, and marginal product will start to fall. Extending the previous analysis on the relationship between average product and average costs to marginal values, we conclude that after diminishing marginal returns set in, the marginal cost of producing the last unit of output rises. Again, we have a pattern of decline and then rise in marginal costs—this time as output expands.

Let's show the relationship between average total cost and marginal total cost graphically, and then explain the pattern of the graph. Figure 4.1 shows that the two curves have the same round U-shape. But the points of major interest are the minimum points of the two curves and their point of intersection.

Note that what are three points conceptually merge into only two graphically, in that the curves intersect at the minimum point of the average cost curve. Before explaining this pattern, we can define point *A* simply as the minimum point on the marginal cost curve. What is the significance of *A*? It is the point of diminishing marginal returns.

Let's approach the marginal-average connection by using an example outside of economics. Suppose a class has 25 students with an individual average weight of 145 pounds. This, you know, means that if we assigned a weight of 145 to each of the 25 students, we would get the same total weight for the class as we would if we added the true individual weights.

Figure 4.1
Average and Marginal Cost Curves.

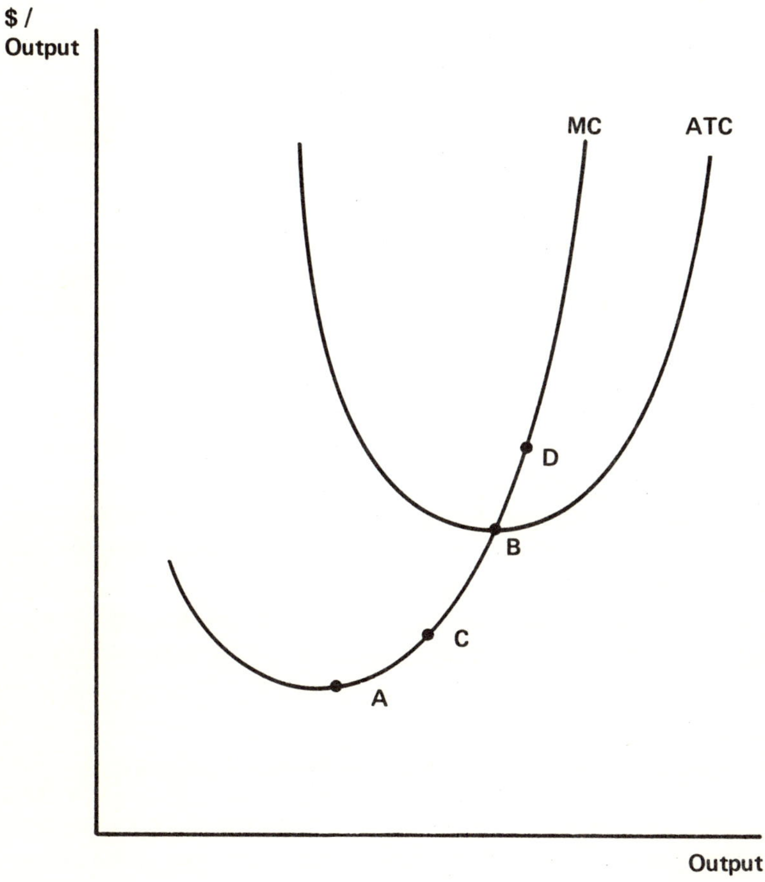

Now let's assume that new students enter the class and that each successive one weighs more than the other, with the 26th student weighing 135 pounds, the 27th weighing 140, and so on. (This assumption is required to make the situation analogous to the cost pattern. That is, we have described a condition of increasing marginal weights at some point when the marginal lies below the average figure.)

The 26th student will pull the average down, because at 135 pounds he is below the previous average of 145 pounds. He won't drag it down much, because he is only one of 26 students contributing to the total weight, and he isn't much below the average.

The 27th student weighs more than the 26th, so marginal weight is increasing. But the important thing to remember is that despite this rise in the marginal value, the average weight is still declining, since 140 pounds is less that 144 pounds, the average after the addition of the 26th student. We have labeled point *C* in Figure 4.1 to show the similar position on the cost curves of a rising marginal cost lying below the average cost, with the average cost falling.

If the next, or 28th, student entering the class weighs just over 144 pounds, the marginal will still be rising; but now it has just reached the level of the average, and will stop pulling it down. The analogous point on the cost curve is *B*, when rising marginal cost and minimum average cost intersect at the output level at which diminishing average returns appear.

The 29th student weighs, say, 150 pounds. The rising marginal exceeds the average and pulls it up. Our analogous point on the cost curve is *D*. Additional heavier students will pull the average up still higher. Note that the marginal cost curve rises more steeply than the average cost curve in Figure 4.1. This follows, since the average is weighted by the *existing* values of the numerous individual units; therefore, the higher value of the marginal unit does not move the average by much, certainly nowhere near as much as it moves its own value.

We have spoken enough about costs at this time. Now we will look at the revenue picture, and then bring costs back in to arrive at the firm's output position to maximize profits.

Average and Marginal Revenue under Perfect Competition

The firm derives its revenue from the sales of its output. Its total revenue is nothing more than its dollar sales, which is the sum of the money received from each unit sold. This sounds like a roundabout, windy way to describe a simple concept, but revenues are only simple under conditions of perfect competition, when each unit sells at the same price no matter how many the firm puts on the market.

Thus, total revenue simply equals the uniform price multiplied by the number of units sold. In symbols,

$$TR = P \times O \tag{5}$$

Average revenue is total revenue per unit of output, or $TR/O = P$. Thus, average revenue is simply the price of the product. As long as all units sell for the same price (this is the usual marketing practice), average revenue equals price, no matter what the degree of competition in the product market.

Marginal revenue is the increase in total revenue from the sale of the last unit to the market. Since competition is assumed perfect, the firm can sell as much as it wants at the same price. Thus, price remains a constant over the entire range, and the addition to revenue from each additional unit sold is nothing more than the price of the product.

The demand curve for its product represents the amount the firm can sell at different prices. Under perfect competition, it can sell nothing at a price above the market price, and would have no incentive to sell at a lower price. Consequently, the demand curve, the average revenue curve, and the marginal revenue curve all lie on the same horizontal, or price, line.

Revenues, Costs and Equilibrium Output

Let's put our cost and revenue curves together, in Figure 4.2. By discussing the significant points on this graph, we can arrive at the firm's output position which will maximize its profits.

Profits can be derived directly from the average cost and average revenue curves. Profits are measured by the difference between average revenue and average cost, multiplied by the output produced and sold. In symbols,

$$\pi = TR - TC \tag{6}$$

(The Greek pi is used for profits to distinguish it from P, the symbol for price.) $TR = AR \times O$ and $TC = ATC \times O$. Thus,

$$\pi = (AR - ATC)\, O$$

Figure 4.2
Unit Costs, Revenue and Equilibrium Output.

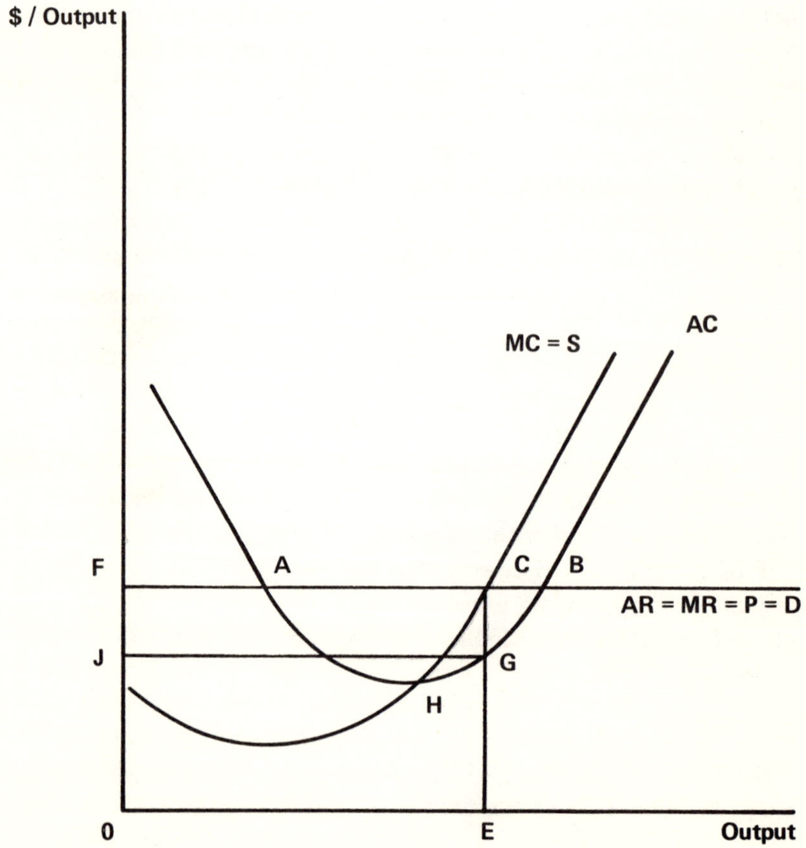

Looking at Figure 4.2, we see that there are two break-even points, *A* and *B*. Between these points, or at output levels greater than *A* but less than *B*, the firm has an opportunity to make profits. Over this range, the average cost curve lies below the average revenue curve. Since the firm tries to maximize profits, it will choose to come up with an output level between *A* and *B*. Our problem is to find out just what this output level will be.

To do this, we will bring the marginal values into the analysis. Note that marginal revenue is a constant, while marginal cost is rising—first lying below the marginal revenue, then crossing it, and then rising above it. Thus, for outputs just a little beyond *A*, the additional total revenue from an extra unit of output, *MR*, exceeds the addition to cost of producing this output, *MC*. As long as this condition holds, it obviously pays for the firm to increase output.

At point *C*, the firm's marginal revenue equals its marginal cost, which means that its addition to revenue from extra output just equals the addition to its costs. This is the profit-maximizing *equilibrium output* of the firm. To go beyond *C* would result in a reduction in profits; with rising marginal costs and constant marginal revenues, the production and sale of higher output would add less to revenues than to costs.

We can now state the fundamental principle of profit maximization for every firm. *The firm maximizes its profits, and thus reaches its equilibrium output, at the level at which marginal cost equals marginal revenue.*

The firm's supply schedule, under perfect competition, can be derived from this principle. The supply curve relates the quantity produced and sold on the market at each price level. We see that the firm's equilibrium output is where marginal cost equals marginal revenue, which, under perfect competition, also results in an equality between marginal cost and price. This equality at equilibrium would hold for all price levels, not just the one price drawn in Figure 4.2. Thus the supply schedule for the firm under perfect competition is represented by its marginal cost curve. Accordingly we add the symbol "S," for supply, to *MC* on the graph.

Let's now show the volume of maximum profits at equilibrium output on the graph. Total revenue, the product of average revenue and output, is *OE x EC*, or the area of the rectangle *OECF*. Total costs, which equal average costs times output, *OE x EG*, is the area of the rectangle *OEGJ*. Then profits are the area of the rectangle *JGCF*. This is the maximum rectangle that can be drawn between average revenue and average costs. The geometry, you should realize, is just here to clarify the economics.

Long-Run Equilibrium for the Firm

We have described a profitable firm. The firm is operating in a perfectly competitive market or industry, where there are many firms producing the same product and earning similar profits. Since the industry is competitive, other firms can easily enter it if they so choose. As a matter of fact, firms currently in other industries or new business units *will be* attracted to this profitable industry, and will increase the industry's total output.

You might ask: Aren't these firms making profits in their own industries? Will only inefficient firms who couldn't make a go of it in other fields be attracted? To answer the question, we must take a closer look at the nature of profits earned by the firm described by Figure 4.2.

Any profits arising from a situation in which average revenues exceed average costs are considered above-normal profits. *Normal profits* equal the average profit rates on investments for all industries. They are implicitly subsumed in the cost schedule of the firm. Designating profits as a cost is not an example of the capriciousness of economic analysis. Recall the concept of opportunity cost. The cost to a firm of putting its investment in Industry A is the profit foregone from investing and producing in Industry B. If we take all investment as a whole, the normal profit-opportunity cost of the firm described by Figure 4.2 is the average profitability of all industries as a whole.

Thus, it is not the inefficient firm that is attracted to the industry of which our firm is a part, the typical firm everywhere earning normal profits. However, don't assume that this attractive force has no limits, or that we are going to reach the ridiculous conclusion that all firms will rush to this industry, so that eventually there will only be one product made in the country. Markets have a way of achieving a balance between supply and demand.

New entrants into the industry swell supply. Although total industry supply cannot be affected by the output policy of any single firm (this is a condition of perfect competition), the increased number of firms supplying output will significantly raise the total supply on the market. With no change in demand, the rise in quantity supplied will depress the market price. We show the effect of expanded supply on market price in Figure 4.3.

Similar to an increase in demand (shown in Figure 2.1 in Chapter 2), an increase in supply, from S to S' as drawn in Figure 4.3, means that there

Figure 4.3
Effect of Increase in Supply on Market Price.

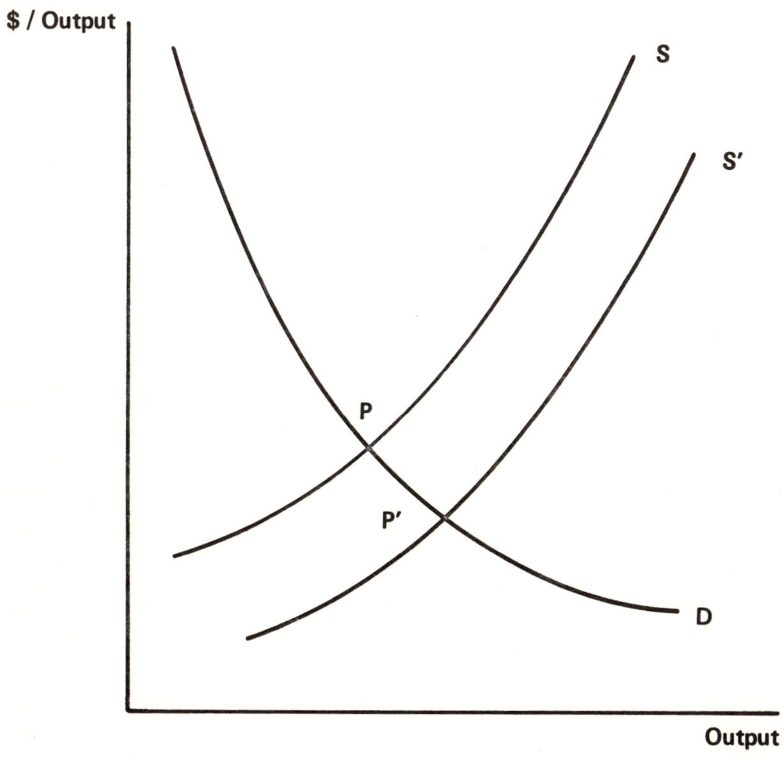

will either be more output at the same price, the same output at a lower price, or a combination of the two. The result of the increase in supply coming from new firms entering the industry is an increase in quantity sold and a decline in price.

The price drop in Figure 4.2 would result in a lower price line. We haven't drawn in a lower line, because the graph is already complicated enough; but it should be clear that a lower product price, with unchanged cost curves, would reduce the rectangle of profit.

Long-run equilibrium will be reached for the industry when above-normal profits are entirely eliminated. This will occur when the price falls to a level just touching the average cost curve. This point of contact, or tangency, will occur at the minimum point, *H*, of the average cost curve. Thus, at long-run equilibrium, output is at the confluence of three curves—the average cost curve, the marginal cost curve, and the price line. Note that this is also the point of maximum productive efficiency, in that costs per unit are at their lowest level.

At equilibrium output for the industry, when the extra profit for the typical firm is eliminated, its output will be cut slightly from its previous above-normal-profit-making level. Since the firm's marginal cost-supply curve is upward sloping, it will meet a lower price at less output. This drop in supply for the individual firm is consistent with a substantial increase in total industry output, however, because there will be more firms in the industry.

If the entire economy were characterized by perfect competition, all industries would be earning the same profit rate on investment in long-run equilibrium, and all firms would be operating at maximum efficiency. The first condition would be met by movement of firms from low to high profit industries to bring about uniform profitability for all industries. The second condition would be reached as less efficient firms would be squeezed out of the market by competitive forces. If they couldn't achieve the low average costs of the typical firm, they would have to lose money by selling at the competitive price. As firms in competitive industries, they would have to meet the market price or drop out of production.

But we know that we do not have a perfectly competitive economic system. Many firms sell in noncompetitive industries because of oligopolistic or product differentiation elements in the product market. Now, let's look at the changes in the analysis of the firm's profit-maximizing output position that arise in imperfectly competitive industries.

Average and Marginal Revenue under Imperfect Competition

The big difference faced by the firm selling in an imperfect market, as compared to the firm selling in a competitive market, is that it cannot sell as much as it wishes at a constant price. Since the firm forms a significant part of the whole market, it is to some extent a price determiner, not simply a price acceptor. Thus, when it sells more units, it noticeably raises market supply and depresses the price. Expressed differently–and more realistically, as market processes go–in order to sell more, the firm must lower its price.

The reverse is also true. If the firm wants to raise the price, it must be prepared to sell less. But a much worse fate would befall the firm in perfect competition that tried to raise its price; such a firm would find its sales falling to zero.

Average revenue would still equal the price of the product. Although the price changes for *every* level of output, *any* level, all units sell at the same price. Therefore, the fundamental equation of revenues, price, and output still applies–that is, $TR = P \times O$ and $AR = P = TR/O$.

Furthermore, the $AR = P$ curve is still the firm's demand curve, revealing the quantity demanded at each price level. But now the marginal revenue curve no longer coincides with the average revenue curve. Recall that marginal revenue is the addition to total revenue from sale of an additional unit of output. For the firm in perfect competition, then, marginal revenue is identical with price, since each additional unit of output sells at the same price.

In the case of a firm selling in an imperfect market, each additional unit of output sells at a lower price. But marginal revenue is less than the price of the last unit sold; following the principle that all units sell at the same price for a given level of output, the price of all the previous units before the last must also fall to the level that enables the additional one to be sold.

Thus, marginal revenue falls because of two factors: first, the last unit must be sold at a lower price–a factor related to the downward slope of the demand schedule; second, the price of the preceding units must fall to this new lower level. This relationship between demand-price and marginal revenue should become clearer with reference to Table 4.1, which presents hypothetical values of output and price for a firm selling in an imperfectly competitive market.

Table 4.1
Hypothetical Output and Price Schedule for a Firm Selling in an Imperfect Market.

P=AR	0	TR	MR	MR
$1.20	5	$6.00	--	--
1.10	6	6.60	$.60	$1.10-5(.10)=$.60
1.00	7	7.00	.40	1.00-6(.10)= .40
.90	8	7.20	.20	.90-7(.10)= .20
.80	9	7.20	.00	.80-8(.10)= .00
.70	10	7.00	-.20	.70-9(.10)= -.20

In this table, we have found the marginal revenue by two methods. In the first *MR* column, we have simply measured the change in total revenue from the addition of one more unit in sales. In the second *MR* column, we have broken down these values into their two components–the addition to total revenue from the last output sold, minus the reduction in revenue from the previous units now sold at a lower price. (Note that there are no marginal revenue values listed for the fifth unit, since we have not recorded the price and total revenue at which four units could be sold.)

We will show the same relationship between average and marginal revenues graphically in Figure 4.4 In this example, we have used a straight line average revenue-price-demand curve. Of course this is not the unique shape of demand curves. All that demand curves for firms selling in imperfect markets have in common is that they slope downward.

The marginal revenue curve lies below the average revenue curve for every level of output–except in the case of the first unit, which is not shown.

At the ninth unit of output, marginal revenue is zero. For the tenth and subsequent unit (not shown), marginal revenue would be negative. In addition, the demand curve would be inelastic after nine units; with a decline in price, total revenue would fall, indicating that the relative gain in quantity sold did not compensate for the relative decline in price.

No rational imperfectly competitive firm would produce and sell at an output at which the demand curve was inelastic. If it wanted to maximize

Figure 4.4
Demand and Marginal Revenue Curves for Firms Selling in an Imperfect Market.

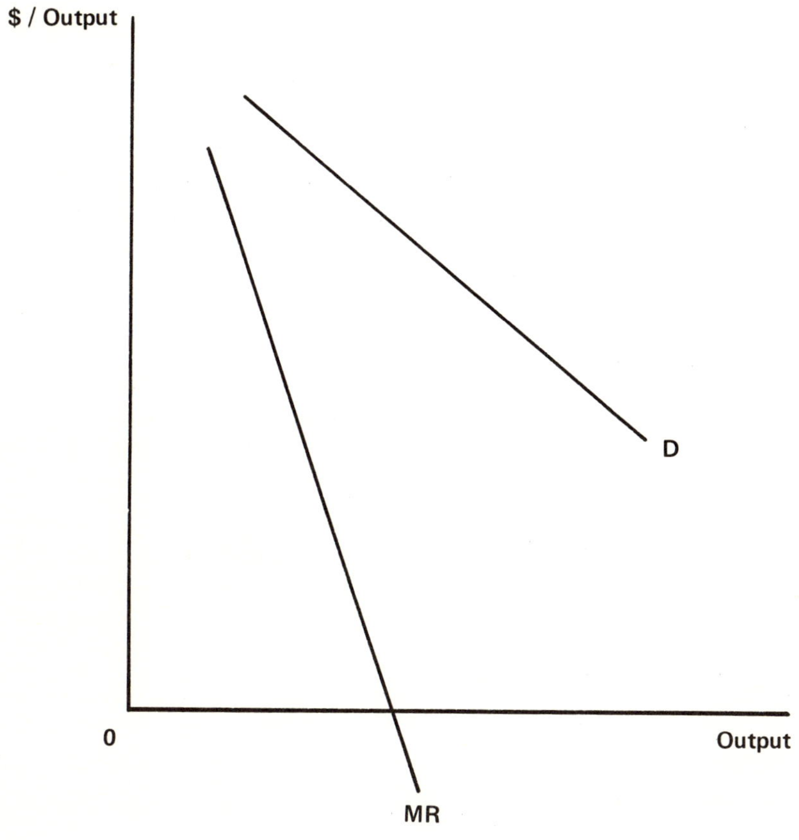

profits, it would not make sense to add an extra unit of sales if revenue *were reduced* by increasing output. To say that the firm would sell at an output in the elastic range of its demand curve is a first step at arriving at its equilibrium, profit-maximizing output. But we can be more precise than that.

Equilibrium Output for the Imperfectly Competitive Firm

The principle we followed in arriving at the equilibrium output for a firm operating under perfect competition still applies in this case. The firm will maximize profits, and will thus choose to produce output at the level at which marginal revenue equals marginal cost. But in the case of the imperfectly competitive firm, marginal revenue is no longer a constant, equal to the price; and, consequently, neither is the marginal cost schedule equal to the firm's supply curve.

Since marginal revenue lies below the price and demand curve, the price the consumer pays for the last unit of the product is less than the firm receives in added revenue from it. Let's look at the equilibrium position shown in Figure 4.5. This graph portrays a situation in which the firm is just earning normal profits. The firm could have been earning above-normal profits; this would have meant that at some output range, average cost would have lain below the average revenue-demand curve.

If above-normal profits are earned by an imperfectly competitive firm, they might persist for a long time. In fact, it is logically questionable to speak of a long-run equilibrium position for the industry, with new firms entering the industry to expand supply and lower price to eliminate above-normal profits. Since the industry is not perfectly competitive, we can assume that it would be difficult for new firms to enter it and take advantage of the potentially high profits. Either the industry is imperfect because the typical firm in it is very large, indicating the need for a greater deal of capital to form a firm competitive with those already established; or the industry is characterized by product differentiation, in which case there would be a great risk to a new firm in getting its product accepted by consumers.

Returning to our graph of a firm just earning normal profits, we see in it two features common to all firms. To repeat, equilibrium output, *OA*, is reached at the intersection of the marginal revenue and marginal cost curves. In addition, the marginal cost curve crosses the average cost curve at the minimum point of the latter.

Figure 4.5
Equilibrium Output for an Imperfectly Competitive Firm.

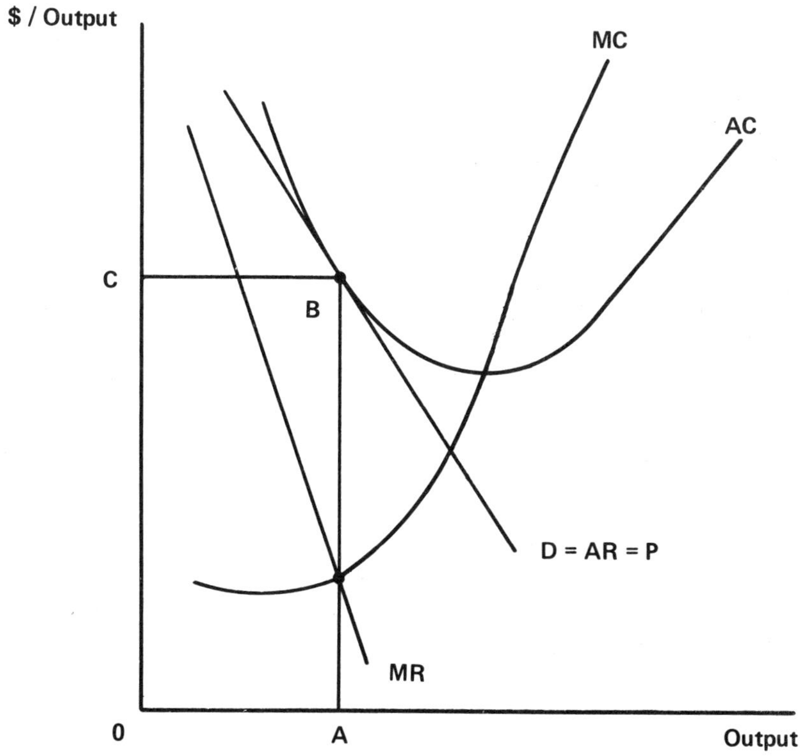

In this case, the best the firm can do is to break even, subsuming the opportunity cost of foregone normal profits in the average cost schedule. At the break-even point, total revenues equal total cost, represented by the area of the rectangle *OABC*.

Note one significant feature of the imperfectly competitive firm. When it is earning normal profits—thus indicating the best allocation of investment funds, in that nothing would be gained by other firms entering the industry; or, expressed more realistically, perhaps, in that nothing would be lost in total profits by the inability of other firms to enter the industry easily—the firm is not operating at maximum efficiency. That is, at equilibrium, the firm is not operating at the minimum point of its average cost curve.

The firm chooses to sell at less than its most efficiently produced output, even though it could reduce unit costs by expanding output. This decision is made because the price, or revenue per unit, would fall even faster than unit costs, as shown in Figure 4.5. Thus, the characteristics of declining price with rising output for the individual firm in an imperfectly competitive industry explain why the typical firm in such an industry does not produce at maximum efficiency.

Critics of monopoly, or of all forms of market imperfection, point out the cost of inefficient production to consumers as an important shortcoming of these types of markets; they do so to justify their attacks on bigness of firms and concentration of industry output among a few sellers. They conclude that if the industry were competitive, with cost curves unaffected by the nature of competition in the product market, the price would fall to the minimum point of the average cost curve as each firm produced at maximum efficiency. This would be the situation at long-run equilibrium for a perfectly competitive industry, with above-normal profits eliminated.

On the other hand, bigness, if not the excess of monopoly, has its defenders. They argue that cost curves are affected by the size of the firm. Big firms have substantial resources which they can devote to research and development. Research can result in new methods of reducing costs, and development can be directed toward product improvement. The effect of these expenditures is to cheapen production or improve quality of output, which can be translated into lower costs or more utility for the consumer at the same price.

Thus, the defenders of bigness argue that the cost curves are lower when the individual firm is large than when it is small. To make the industry competitive would take more effort than having a chartist redo the curves. Effective attempts to reduce the size of the typical firm would have to be made in order to reduce its market share to insignificance. (Note that this argument does not carry much weight for industries which are imperfectly competitive because of market differentiation.)

In effect, the defenders of bigness are arguing that, in theory, the product price *would be* reduced if the industry were competitive with the cost curves as drawn. But, in fact, they say, these curves are what they are because the firms *are* big. It is not the result of market imperfection in itself that they find beneficial to the consumer, but the circumstances that lead to imperfection–big, low-cost firms which lead to low prices even when these firms do not produce at maximum efficiency.

Which side is right? The fact that the argument still continues implies that the question is a difficult one to answer.

Summary

Unlike the individual, who has to weigh the cost of extra effort to increase his earnings and who therefore reaches his best utility position at less than maximum earnings, the firm can have profit maximization as its goal, since earning more profit takes no more effort on the part of those responsible for administering the firm. Profit maximization requires production at that level of output at which the difference between revenue and costs is at a minimum.

Costs are included in two classes: fixed costs and variable costs. Fixed costs are unrelated to output over a given range of output and for a finite time period. The output-range limitation arises because if output were projected to rise or fall significantly and to persist at the new level, the firm would find it could produce more effectively at a higher or lower scale of operations, or volume of fixed factors. The time limitation is related to the scale influence, but it also has an independent effect. For example, if the firm were losing money at even the most efficient scale, it would eventually reduce its fixed costs to zero–that is, go out of business. Since total fixed costs are unrelated to the volume of output, within limits, average fixed costs decline as output expands.

Variable costs are those which are incurred in using variable factors along with the fixed ones to make the firm's product. Total variable costs increase with output, but average costs decline with output increases at very low levels of production and employment of variable factors. Eventually, diminishing returns from the employment of additional units of variable factors to work with fixed factors set in, and average costs then rise with output over the rest of the output range.

Diminishing returns also explain the U-shape of the marginal cost curve, which is the schedule of the additions to total cost from increasing output by one unit. Changes in marginal cost affect average cost. When the marginal cost lies below the average cost, average cost continues to fall even if marginal cost is rising. When the marginal cost exceeds the average cost, the latter rises; and marginal cost exactly equals average cost at the minimum point of the average cost curve.

Now, as to revenues: for a firm operating in a perfectly competitive product market, price is constant over its entire output range. Marginal revenue equals price. The firm maximizes its profits by producing at the output at which marginal cost equals marginal revenue, or price. The marginal cost curve then represents the firm's supply curve.

Normal profits for the firm equal the average profits earned by the economy as a whole. Since these profits are foregone by the firm engaging in the enterprise in question, they are an opportunity cost to the firm; as such, they are included in the firm's fixed and average cost curves. Firms may earn above-normal profits for a time, but the high profits would attract other firms to this industry. When these firms entered the industry, they would expand market supply, thus reducing product price and eventually eliminating all above-normal profits. In long-run equilibrium, with all firms earning normal profits, each would be producing at maximum efficiency (at the output for which average costs are at a minimum) the output of the emergence of diminishing average returns (the output at which marginal costs equal average costs).

The results are more complex for firms selling in imperfect product markets. These firms cannot sell all they want at a constant price, but face a downward sloping demand curve as price declines with greater output.

Although the average revenue, price, and demand schedules are the same, marginal revenue for these firms lies below average revenue. Marginal revenue falls not only because the price of the additional unit is less than the price at which the preceding units could have been sold, but also because the price at which the previous output could be sold falls, too.

As in the case of perfect competition, the firm in an imperfect market will produce at the output at which marginal cost equals marginal revenue. But in this case, the price paid by the purchaser for the last unit exceeds the addition to the firm's revenue from the sale.

If the firm in an imperfect market simply earns normal profits, it will be producing at less than maximum efficiency. Such a firm could reduce average costs by expanding output, but in so doing it would reduce its average revenue even more.

That market imperfection leads to built-in inefficiency makes many analysts argue against bigness as such, when concentration of production leads to market imperfection. Defenders of bigness argue that although imperfectly competitive large firms produce at less than their maximum productive efficiency, they can sell their product at lower prices than if the industry were made competitive by fragmenting production among many small firms.

Chapter Five The Firm as Demander of Factors of Production

In pursuit of profit maximization, the firm not only takes pains to sell its product on the most advantageous terms, but also keeps in mind the various costs that arise at its maximum-profit output. In the last chapter, we looked at costs in the sense of relating them to different levels of output. In this chapter, we will look more deeply into costs.

Whatever the volume of output, the firm will try to produce its goods as cheaply as possible. Since there are several combinations of factors it can use to produce a given output, the firm will have to consider the productivity of each factor when used in conjunction with others in production, along with their prices, to reach its least cost combination. If this all sounds very complicated, don't despair; admittedly, the analysis is not the easiest to follow.

To simplify matters, we will only consider two factors of production. We will assume that they can substitute for each other, to a degree, in production. Furthermore, we will assume that the firm is an unimportant demander of each; therefore, as it varies its demand for these factors in its pursuit of the least cost combination for producing a given level of output, it does not affect their market prices.

Finding the amount of labor demanded by the firm at the given labor price (wage level) permits us to locate a point on the firm's labor demand schedule. Then we derive the labor demand schedule itself by relating labor inputs demanded to different wage levels. Finally we will discuss market demand, supply, and employment of labor.

The Production Function and Factor Substitutability

If labor and capital can substitute for each other in production, the same volume of output can be produced in many different ways, even when we artificially limit the factors to two. We can use a lot of labor and a little capital, or vice versa, or a moderate amount of both. Even at this stage, we can see that the cost of the factors plays an important part in the firm's decision as to what factors to use. If labor is very cheap compared to capital, the firm will tend to use a factor mix that contains a great deal of labor and little capital. But let's not jump ahead; later in the chapter, we will be able to give a more precise description of the role of relative factor prices in determining factors' employment.

If we add to any factor of production without reducing the employment of another, output will rise—that is, the marginal product of any factor is greater than zero.

The relationship between output and the inputs that produce it is customarily presented as a production function. In symbols, with L standing for man hours of labor, and K for machine hours of capital, $O = f(L,K)$. A functional relationship here simply means that if the firm uses each of its factors most efficiently, output will be exactly determined by the units of capital and labor used in production. Note that we haven't yet said a word about the prices of the factors. There are no dollar signs anywhere in the production function. It is strictly a physical or product engineering description of output resulting from different combinations of inputs.

As long as we are on the subject of the physical aspects of production, let's examine the role of substitutability in the production function. Labor has certain characteristics useful in production, and so does capital. Substitutability means that each factor has some attributes of the other. Speaking less theoretically, each factor can at least to some extent serve in place of the other in production.

This feature of substitutability explains why marginal product does not reach zero as we add more of one factor with the other remaining fixed. According to our discussion in the last chapter, we expect diminishing returns to set in as we keep adding more units of a variable factor to work in cooperation with a fixed amount of another factor. But as long as, say, labor has even some of the characteristics of capital, we are in effect adding certain of the attributes of capital when we add labor. Thus, the marginal product of labor will not fall to zero as we add more units of labor to a fixed amount of capital, because, insofar as production potential is concerned, we are really not keeping all the qualities of capital fixed.

Let's look at the extreme case of perfect factor substitutability. This means that units of labor possess all the attributes of capital; if we add a unit of labor, we are in effect adding a given quantity of the productive qualities of labor. Then, whenever we add a unit of labor, we are really adding a combination of labor and capital that is the same as the existing ratio of the two factors in production. Consequently, the marginal product of labor would not fall as the number of units of labor was increased, because the ratio of the variable to the fixed factor would really not change.

For an analogous example of perfect substitution, suppose you wanted to mail a letter. You could use an eight-cent stamp or two four-cent stamps. If a heavy letter required sixteen-cents postage, adding two four-cent stamps would do the job just as well as adding an eight-cent stamp. The "marginal productivity" of a four-cent stamp has not fallen. But won't the envelope get very crowded with stamps? If thirty-two-cents postage were required, it might become quite a feat to fit eight four-cent stamps on it, especially those of the large commemorative variety. Production problems of the same type might arise in concentrating production on one factor, even when there is perfect substitution among factors. But this is no place for going into tricky analysis.

In fact, let's not deal with extreme cases, but concentrate on the usual productive relationship between factors. In general, we can conclude that the more we add to one factor (the other being fixed), the more its marginal product would tend to fall, but it would not reach zero as long as we allow for some substitutability. Therefore, the more we employ of one factor and the less of another, the higher the marginal product of the second relative to the first.

Factor Cost Ratios and Equilibrium Factor Proportions

Knowing the physical relationship between output and the employment of factors in varying proportions is only part of the story in determining the combination of factors a firm will use in producing a given output. In addition, the firm will have to include the factor's relative prices in deciding the factor combination it will use.

We can approach our analysis by restating the fundamental principle of profit maximization with reference to factor inputs instead of product output. The firm will employ any factor of production in an amount at which the marginal revenue from the last unit employed equals the marginal cost. For labor,

$$MR_L = MC_L \tag{1}$$

and for capital

$$MR_K = MC_K \tag{1a}$$

at the equilibrium employment of each.

For either factor, the marginal revenue is the increase in total revenue resulting from the employment of the last unit. In a perfectly competitive product market, the marginal revenue equals the marginal product contributed by this unit multiplied by the price of the product. Thus, in symbols, for labor, $MR_L = MP_L \times P$; and for capital, $MR_K = MP_K \times P$.

If factor markets are perfectly competitive, and the firm pays the same price for all the units of a factor it hires, no matter how many, the marginal cost of labor is simply the wage rate, w, and the marginal cost of capital, k, is simply the hourly cost of a unit of capital. Therfore, equations (1) and (1a) can be rewritten in expanded form.

$$MP_L \times P = w \tag{2}$$

and

$$MP_K \times P = k \tag{2a}$$

The price term appears in both equations, so that they can be set equal to each other.

$$\frac{w}{MP_L} = \frac{k}{MP_K} = P \text{ or } \frac{MP_L}{MP_K} = P \tag{3}$$

Equation (3) tells us that for equilibrium employment of the two factors, to produce a given level of output most cheaply, their relative costs are set equal to their relative marginal products.

If their relative prices are given, the firm will hire the factors in combination until the marginal products come into equality with the price ratio. For example, if a man-hour of labor costs \$3.00–that is, if the wage is \$3.00–and a machine hour of capital costs \$6.00, labor and capital would be hired in a combination at which the marginal product of capital is twice that of labor.

It is easy to see that any other combination to produce the same output would be costlier. If the initial combination used "too little" capital relative to labor, such that the marginal product of capital were three times that of labor, then six dollars taken away from labor cost and applied to capital would reduce man-hours employed by two and increase machine-hours of capital by one unit; this would result in an increase in output. Expressed in terms of producing the same output, if six dollars were taken away from labor costs, less than six dollars to purchase less than one full machine-hour of capital would be all that was needed to maintain the level of output.

In the absence of easy and costless movement of factors, differences in factor price arise between countries and even between regions of the same country. Assuming universal identity of production functions, relative factor prices are strongly affected by their relative supply in particular areas. Countries which have abundant labor and little capital would therefore tend to specialize in production of goods which are labor intensive. But substitutability is not characteristic for production methods of all goods.

Take the case of Oriental rugs. For centuries these have been made in Iran. For generations, workers have been trained by their families in the art and techniques required. Though requiring skill and talent, the work is very arduous, harmful to the vision, and generally unpleasant. Except for a plentiful wool supply, practically the only factor required in production is this specialized labor.

With economic development in Iran, many low-paid workers in this industry have found other employment opportunities elsewhere; therefore, the wage that would keep them engaged in rug-making has been bid up.

Our textbooks tell us these workers should be replaced by machines; and, in fact, for many years we have manufactured an artistic and grammatical abomination called an American Oriental. But, in truth, there is no machine-made substitute for the real thing—the beauty and distinction of which lies in its hand-craftsmanship.

What then has been the effect on the industry? Rising production costs have practically priced the good out of the market. There is now some production in Afghanistan; this country, with its lower stage of economic development and wages, is increasing its share of the Persian rug market. Without the possibility of much factor substitution, though, the industry's supply schedule has shifted to the left, making for much higher prices and sharply reduced production.

Take aircraft production as another example of an industry having poor factor substitution. Production in the United States used a great deal of capital and highly skilled and trained labor, which are factors in relative abundance here. Brazil does not have a large supply of these factors, but it does have a great deal of unskilled labor. Does it then produce planes with production methods vastly different from those used here, employing a lot of inexpensive labor and little capital and few skilled workers? Of course not. Raw manpower is a poor substitute for machines and a trained work force in aircraft production; and no matter how cheap the unskilled labor is, it would be more costly to produce planes by stressing this factor. Brazil simply doesn't produce planes at all.

Consider the production of artificial flowers. Admittedly, this isn't the type of industry on which great economies are based. But it is a good example of an industry having easy factor substitutability. For years American and Japanese producers competed for the consumer's artificial-flower dollar, with each country using vastly different production methods. The Japanese handmade product was certainly more artistically fashioned, but the American machine-made good offered strong competition.

But now Japan's economy is very advanced; its industrial productivity has grown, and its wages have increased. The handmade flowers would have to be sold at a much higher price, reflecting increased labor costs, the chief ingredient of production. You have probably guessed the adjustment that was made in Japanese production. Horror of horrors, they are now selling machine-made flowers, too, and competing very nicely! Don't lament the loss of the old-fashioned skills, the loss of artisanship in work. Their decline measures the economic strength of a country. Ask the

Japanese worker which he prefers: the "good old days" of tedious craftsmanship at a bare subsistence pay, or the modern system of separation of the worker from the product at high wages.

Let's look at one last example concerning factor substitution. Until about 50 years ago, the textile industry was concentrated in New England. This industry characteristically uses much low-cost labor, as opposed to skilled labor or capital. Therefore, when wage levels tended to rise in New England because of rapid economic development in the area, and perhaps also because of successful union wage pressure, the industry moved to the South, where unskilled labor was abundant, cheap, and unorganized.

But the new mills in the South were built with the most modern machinery and equipment, including much labor-saving, or labor-substituting, capital. At first view, the practice might seem irrational—moving to an area to take advantage of lower wages and then, in effect, substituting capital for labor. Closer examination reveals an economic method to this madness. Labor still is an important ingredient in textile production, but new technology has made factor substitution towards capital a more economical means of production. However, if the industry were presently located in the North, it would still pay it to move to the South to allow a reduction in labor costs.

Labor Demand for a Firm

Our method of analysis should now be familiar to you. Having explained the equilibrium distribution of factors in production at given factor prices, we have really explained one point on the labor demand curve. To derive the whole demand curve, we will simply show the response of the quantity of labor demanded to a change in its price (wage), keeping fixed the underlying determinants of labor demand.

What are the basic factors determining labor demand at any price? They are the amount of output the firm wishes to produce, the physical or productive efficiency of labor, and the price of capital. To see the degree of parallelism between product and factor demand, let's repeat the basic factors determining consumer demand for a particular product. These are income, tastes, and the price of substitutes. If we stretch the meaning of these terms a little, we find a very close relationship between the basic determinants of product and factor demand. Let's take them one at a time.

Income and Production Level

How much we demand of any product is greatly influenced by our purchasing power. As our income rises, we buy more of all goods, except the few "inferior" ones. Similarly, the demand for any factor of production depends heavily on the amount of output the firm produces. Consequently, the demand for a factor rises when production does.

Thus, production to a firm is very close to income for the consumer in its effect on demand. The analogy is not perfect though, since it is very difficult to think of a counterpart to an inferior good—that is, a factor of production the use of which tends to decline as production rises.

Tastes and Productive Efficiency

We have to strain a little to find a close analogy between tastes for the consumer and physical productivity for the firm as elements influencing demand. Tastes refer to the subjective attitudes of the consumer toward particular goods. A chance in taste toward a good leads to an increase in utility from each unit of it, and tends to strengthen demand for the product.

There is nothing subjective about physical productivity. It is strictly an engineering concept. It refers to the ability of a factor of production to produce output in conjunction with other factors of production. But if a new technique, invention, or process raises the productivity of the factor, demand for it will increase. Here we see one strong conceptual similarity between consumer taste and factor efficiency. Each is the single element in determination of demand, whether of the consumer or of the firm, which relates to the characteristics of the good, or factor, in question. Income or production levels are *outside* forces influencing demand; so too are the prices of substitutes which form the third basic determinant of demand.

Price of Substitutes

Demand for the product moves directly with the price of substitutes. Remember the butter-oleo example. If the price of oleo rises, the demand for butter increases. The effect of the price of substitutes on factor demand is identical. If the price of capital rises, the demand for labor increases. In fact, under our simplified assumption of a two-factor world, we could analyze the demand schedule of labor by keeping its price constant and examining the changes in quantity of labor demanded in response to the changes in the price of capital. Then, a rise in the price of capital would lead to a relative wage decline and an increase in the amount of labor demanded. That we could not analyze the price movements of *one* substitute alone in studying the demand for a particular product does not indicate a weakness in the analogy of the effects of prices of substitutes on product, compared with factor demand, but the lack of realism in our assumption of a two-factor world.

In the real economic sense of the term, there are many factors of production. Within the labor group itself, there are skilled and unskilled workers. In fact each occupation to some extent constitutes a separate factor of production, if we use this term to signify a somewhat homogeneous group of individual units of production that can be increased or reduced in size to counter a reduction or increase in the use of a different homogeneous group of productive units in producing a given level of output.

Now, let's get down to the business of deriving the firm's demand curve for labor. As with all such schedules, the curve refers to the quantity demanded at a moment in time at different price (wage) levels. The instantaneous nature of the curve means that production level, productivity of labor, and price of capital are given, and are thus unrelated to the wage level at that moment.

To begin, let's repeat equation (3), showing the initial equilibrium position of the firm in its employment of factors.

$$\frac{w}{MP_L} = \frac{k}{MP_K} \qquad (3)$$

Now suppose there is a wage increase. The immediate effect is to disturb the equilibrium position. The ratio of wages to marginal physical product of labor has risen relative to the ratio of the cost of a machine-hour to the original physical product of capital.

To reach a new equilibrium position, the firm will reduce its costs by substituting capital for labor. Two points about this substitution must be made clear. In the first place, substitution does not occur easily or quickly. In some cases, union contractual terms may prevent the substitution. In others, the machinery to bring about the substitution may not be available or perhaps not even invented yet. Then, too, machinery comes in lumpy units; therefore, it might not pay to make the substitution. But in any case, the pressure for substitution is there; and in the long run, it will probably be made.

The second point requiring clarification refers to the statement that the firm will reduce costs by making the substitution. Of course, it will not produce more cheaply than it did before the wage increase. Logic argues against this; for if it could produce more cheaply now that the price of one of the factors has risen, it was obviously not producing at its equilibrium—its most inexpensive combination of factors—before. (There is perhaps some basis to a very long-term argument that higher wages stimulate invention of new and more efficient machines, but we are implicitly assuming a constant technology in our analysis.) The costs, then, that are reduced by the substitution are those at the new high level that would be reached because wages rose.

For those who like their analysis in scientific rather than economic terms, we can say that when an equilibrium position is disturbed, the forces at work adjust to restore the equilibrium. In the case of equation (3), the numerator of the left-hand term has risen and thus increased its fraction. The other three elements then begin to work to restore the balance. The left-hand term's denominator rises to try to reduce the fraction, while the numerator of the right-hand term rises and its denominator falls to raise that fraction towards the higher left-hand fraction.

But sticking to economic analysis, we get the same results. When the price of labor rises, the demand for its substitute, capital, increases, thus raising the price of capital, k. With greater employment of capital relative to labor, the marginal productivity of capital falls and the marginal productivity of labor rises. In fact, we can make a simple, if facetious, recommendation to labor to increase its productive efficiency. Just ask for a wage increase. (Marginal) productivity will rise, but at the cost of unemployment.

We now get the picture of the labor demand schedule. It is a typical downward sloping curve, with quantity of labor demanded moving inversely to the price (wage rate). As wages rise, capital is substituted for labor; and as wages fall, the substitution goes in the other direction.

Although the above analysis obviously has not led to the following two important conclusions, it can easily be seen that (1) the downward slope of the labor demand schedule depends on the appearance of diminishing returns, and (2) the elasticity of demand depends on the rapidity with which returns diminish, or on factor substitutability.

To explain these conclusions, let's look at equation (2) again. The firm will hire labor up to the point where

$$MP_L \times P = w \tag{2}$$

If the wage falls, the quantity of labor demanded will increase until MP_L falls by the same relative amount. Remember, product price is constant. MP_L falls because of diminishing returns. If diminishing returns do not set in, and if, say, MP_L remains constant no matter how much labor is hired, the labor demand schedule would be infinitely elastic. For any wage decline, the quantity of labor hired would expand without limit.

But the extent of diminishing returns depends on factor substitutability. In the other extreme case of fixed proportion in production, a wage decline would not increase the quantity of labor demanded at all; the demand curve would be perfectly inelastic, since with no substitutability in production possible, the marginal product of an additional unit of labor would be zero. Obviously, labor demand schedules characteristically fit neither extreme position. There is *some* factor substitutability, and diminishing returns do set in. But the more easily labor can be substituted for capital, the greater is the increase in the quantity of labor demanded in response to a wage decrease, the more gently downward sloping is the labor demand schedule, and the greater is its elasticity.

Elasticity of labor demand is important to union wage policy. If demand is elastic, the union must face the possibility, at least in the long run, of serious negative employment effects from wage increases gained through collective bargaining.

Note the close parallelism between the firm's demand schedule for labor and its product supply schedule. In the last chapter, we found that the latter rose with output expansion consequent to price increases because of diminishing returns. Here we find that the labor demand curve falls because of expanding quantity demanded in response to a lower wage, and also because of diminishing returns.

We also concluded that the marginal cost schedule was the firm's supply schedule, since the firm produced output until it equated marginal cost with marginal revenue (price), and the supply schedule is nothing more than the quantity supplied at each price. Furthermore, we found that this was not the case for imperfect competition; at equilibrium output, marginal cost still equaled marginal revenue, but marginal revenue was lower than price.

In a close analogy to these product-supply characteristics, the marginal revenue schedule $(MP_L \times P)$ is the firm's labor demand schedule, since the firm hires labor until it equates its marginal revenue with marginal cost (wage), and the labor demand schedule is nothing more than the quantity demanded at each wage. This relationship also only applies under perfect competition in the factor market.

Although we are not analyzing conditions of imperfect competition in the product market here, suffice it to say that if the firm had to raise wages as it increased its work force, the marginal cost of labor to it would lie above the wage (the explanation for this is the same as that presented in explaining why marginal revenue lies below average revenue or price under imperfect product market conditions.) Therefore, although the firm buying labor in an imperfect market would still hire labor until its marginal revenue equaled its marginal cost, the marginal cost would exceed the wage, and the marginal revenue schedule would no longer represent the firm's labor demand schedule.

Market Labor Demand and Supply

It is not a complicated step to move from the labor demand schedule of a single firm to the demand schedule for the market as a whole. Here, though, we note a significant difference in aggregation from the summation of schedules of individual firms in the product market.

There we spoke of the sum of individual firms' supply of a particular product, so that the market supply curve really referred to an industry schedule. But in considering the total demand for a particular type of labor, or occupational classification, we cut across industry lines. Nevertheless, the process of aggregation is familiar. As the wage falls, the demand for individual firms increases; and new firms might enter production, in whatever industries, because of lowered production costs.

Although this chapter deals with labor demand, in order to examine the market situation, we should introduce the market supply schedule for a particular type of labor. In any case, if we want to discuss wage levels, we must consider supply; no price is determined by demand alone.

The supply schedule of a particular labor class is conventionally upward sloping, at least it is so in the long run. We settled this point in Chapter 3, but let's review the explanation here. The individual worker may have a backward-bending labor supply schedule, so that at high wages he would offer less labor in response to a wage increase. But this does not mean that in his choice of work settings he would not prefer a higher to a lower wage.

Therefore, if wages rise in occupation A, those currently in it may choose to work less, but workers from other fields will be attracted to it. Of course, this will take time, but it is safe to conclude that, in general, this effect would outweigh the possible negative effect on supply of the negative slope to the individual schedules.

We are thus left with a very conventional market situation indeed—an upward sloping supply schedule and a downward sloping demand schedule. We show this market situation in Figure 5.1. The graph is simple enough, but it is presented here mainly to show the effect of policy efforts to interfere with this classic example of the market mechanism at work. We have in mind the effect on wages and employment of the establishment of minimum wages.

Before the minimum is established, the graph indicates a market wage of *0A*, with employment at *0B*. The total wage bill to the producers, or wage income to the workers, is *0AWB*.

Now suppose a minimum wage is established at *0C*. Minimum wages are not designed to hurt the workers covered. They were initially set by legislation over 30 years ago, and have since been raised many times for the purpose of increasing the incomes of those at the lowest end of the earnings scale. We set minimum wages not only by law, but also by custom. Our society frowns upon allowing remunerative effort at jobs which provide less than the minimum wage for noncovered workers. Pressure for higher minimum wages comes not only from those currently at that minimum, and from unions which idealistically are concerned with the welfare of all who work and which, less altruistically, see a rise in the minimum as a force to push their own members' wages up still further, but also from society as a whole, which feels that those who work should at least be able to earn a living wage.

But leaving the motivation for the establishment of minimum wages behind, let's look at the effect. Setting a minimum above the market level reduces the labor demand from *0B* man-hours to *0E*. Supply, on the other hand, increases to *0F*. At first view, it might seem strange to argue that supply will expand; although the market wage level is exceeded, those earning the minimum will still be at the bottom end of the wage scale. But all workers are not covered by minimum wages. Some jobs pay even less—e.g., domestic service as compared with unskilled factory work in many

Figure 5.1
Effect of Minimum Wages and Employment

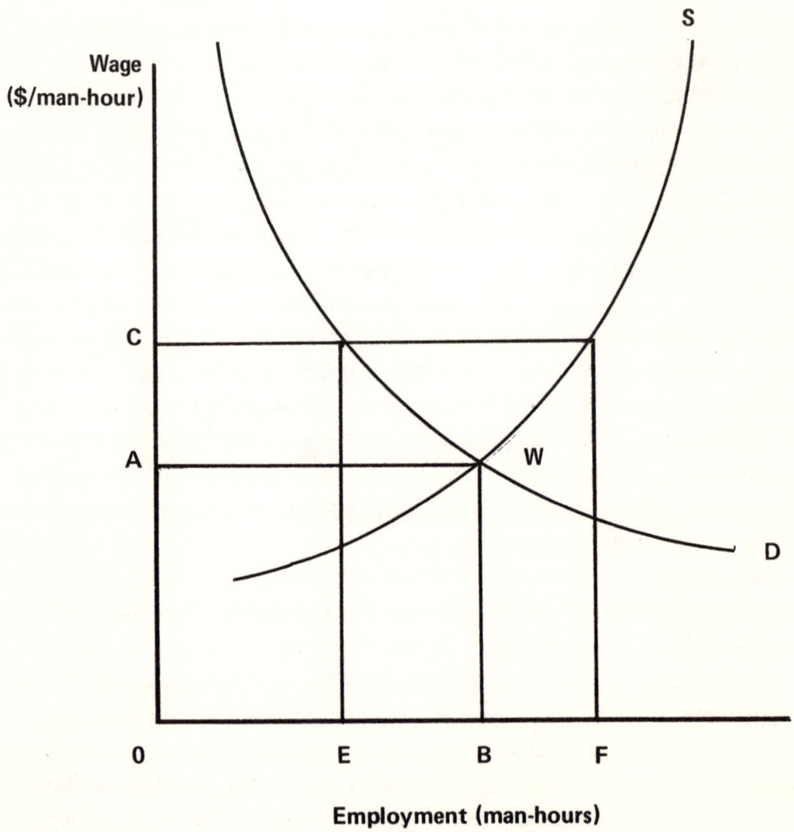

instances. Furthermore, those with little skill or training who are currently not in the labor force might be attracted to the unskilled work force by the higher wage. We can conclude, then, that the upward sloping supply schedule drawn in Figure 5.1 fits the real world.

Wages *do* rise to *OC*. But the harmful side effects of the attainment of a wage increase may make the entire minimum-wage program of questionable benefit to the workers it was intended to assist. Since supply has expanded and demand shrunk, unemployment rises to a point equal to *EF* on the graph. In fact, if the market demand schedule for the affected workers is elastic, their total wage income will decline. Remember that if demand is elastic, a rise in the price (wage rate) results in a decrease in revenue (total labor income). Of course, the harmful employment effects of a minimum wage above the market level could be eased by a rise in unemployment benefits. But this opens up a whole new issue of the effect of nonwork transfer payments on work incentives, the cost in taxes of such a program, etc.

This is not the place to expand on other applications of the analysis presented. The book on microeconomics in this series is concerned exclusively with applications, not only of the points on factor demand raised in this chapter, but of all aspects of the market system as well.

Summary

The firm will try to produce any level of output it decides upon at the least possible cost. To arrive at the lowest production cost, the firm must consider not only the productivities of the various factors but also their relative prices.

In a two-factor system, with labor and capital as the two factors used in production, the least-cost combination will result when factor prices are proportional to their respective marginal products. Expressed differently, this combination is achieved when the ratio of the wage to labor's marginal product is equal to the ratio of the cost of a machine-hour of capital to the marginal product of capital.

Given factor prices, this equilibrium, lowest-cost combination in effect locates one point on the firm's labor demand curve. The elements underlying this demand schedule are the level of production, labor productivity, and the price of the substitute factor (capital). These elements are conceptually similar to the basic determinants of consumer product demand—income, tastes, and the price of substitutes.

The labor demand schedule is downward sloping. With a fall in wages, the equilibrium balance between marginal revenue (the product price multiplied by the marginal productivity of labor) and marginal cost (the wage) is disturbed. More labor will be hired, until the marginal revenue of the last worker is again equal to the new lower wage. The marginal revenue of additional units of labor falls because of diminishing returns. Thus, diminishing returns explain the downward slope of the labor demand curve.

Diminishing returns also account for the upward slope of the firm's product supply schedule. Under perfect competition, the firm's marginal cost curve is also its product supply curve; parallel to this fact, the marginal revenue schedule of labor represents the firm's labor demand curve. This relationship does not hold for either product supply or factor demand under imperfect market conditions.

The prevailing wage rate for a particular occupation is determined by market supply as well as by market demand. The market curves are conventionally downward sloping for labor demand and upward sloping for labor supply, with the market wage determined at the point at which the two curves intersect. The establishment of a minimum wage above the market level will increase the wages of those at the lowest end of the wage scale, but it will also have a harmful effect on them in that wages set above the market level will lead to unemployment. In fact, the practice of setting a minimum wage provides a clear example of the disequilibriating effects of preventing a market from functioning normally in a general market system. Either shortages or, as in this case, surpluses arise when a price is arbitrarily set at variance with the market price. But now we are back to the beginning of the book.

